NEW OXFORD ENGLISH SERIES
General Editor: A. NORMAN JEFFARES

HOPKINS

SELECTIONS

Chosen and edited by

GRAHAM STOREY

FELLOW OF TRINITY HALL, CAMBRIDGE
AND UNIVERSITY LECTURER IN ENGLISH

OXFORD UNIVERSITY PRESS

1967

Oxford University Press, Ely House, London W.1

GLASGOW NEW YORK TORONTO MELBOURNE WELLINGTON
CAPE TOWN SALISBURY IBADAN NAIROBI LUSAKA ADDIS ABABA
BOMBAY CALCUTTA MADRAS KARACHI LAHORE DACCA
KUALA LUMPUR HONG KONG TOKYO

Printed in Great Britain by
The Camelot Press Ltd., London and Southampton

ACKNOWLEDGEMENTS

I am most grateful to Professor W. H. Gardner and Professor N. H. Mackenzie for their generosity in allowing me access, before publication, to their Fourth Edition of *The Poems of G. M. Hopkins* (Oxford, 1967).

I should also like to thank my friends Fr. Illtud Evans, O.P., and Mr. Christopher Parry, for reading the Introduction and Notes and for their helpful suggestions.

May 1966   G. S.

CONTENTS

VERSE

INTRODUCTION

I. LIFE

GERARD MANLEY HOPKINS, the eldest of nine children, was born on 28 July 1844 in Stratford, Essex, into a prosperous, cultivated and unusually talented family. His father, Manley Hopkins, head of a London firm of average adjusters concerned with marine assurance, and later Consul-General for Hawaii, published three volumes of unremarkable Victorian verse—one of them dedicated to Thomas Hood—besides several books on his profession and a history of Hawaii; he was interested in music and psychology and had a passion for word-play and puns. Gerard's mother was the daughter of a successful doctor, who had been a fellow-student of Keats. Both parents were deeply religious High Anglicans. Several uncles and aunts were accomplished in music and drawing, in both of which the young Hopkins showed considerable skill from an early age. Another uncle wrote pious verse. Two of his brothers became professional artists.

In 1852 the family moved to Hampstead, and two years later Hopkins was sent to Highgate School. At Highgate he established himself as a precocious scholar and wrote his first poems. They show some influence of Tennyson, but the dominant feeling is Keatsian. With *The Escorial*—a set piece in Spenserian stanzas—he won the school Poetry Prize in 1860. *A Vision of Mermaids* (1862) he illustrated with a remarkable Blake-like drawing. In February 1863 his *Winter with the*

Gulf Stream (p. 37) appeared in the weekly journal, *Once a Week*.

R. W. Dixon (see p. 205), who taught at Highgate in 1861, remembered Hopkins as 'a pale young boy, very light and active, with a very meditative & intellectual face'. He was very slight and at school was nicknamed 'Skin'. But this physical slightness was already combined with an unusual strength of will. The story of how he once went for a week without drinking any liquids, for a bet, has been often told. In 1863 he won an Exhibition to Balliol and went up to Oxford to read Classics that April.

At Oxford Hopkins thrived. He had had no love for his schooldays; but 'not to love my University would be to undo the very buttons of my being', he later wrote to Alexander Baillie. He made many friends; his letters are full of high spirits. Jowett, then a tutor at Balliol, regarded him as the best classical scholar of his year. His Oxford diaries show a mind excited with new experience, intensely curious and experimental, extraordinarily varied in its energy. They show how widely he read, particularly in the English poets; they are full of lists, derivations, and meanings of words in several languages,[1] which throw much light on his later poetic experiments; of drafts of poems, single lines, beginnings of an epic, of a play; full too of detailed observation of objects that excited him: the colour and formation of flowers and trees, the precise shape and texture of clouds, the exact way in which water bubbles and surges as it rushes over a weir (p. 111). They contain also numerous minute, beautifully-drawn pencil sketches, mainly of the details of medieval churches and cathedrals. He was, he told Baillie, sketching 'a good deal' now, in a 'Ruskinese' manner. This was in September 1863, and the following July he wrote to him: 'I have now

[1] See pp. 111–12 for examples.

a more rational hope than before of doing something—in poetry and painting.'

For most of his first two years at Oxford aesthetic interests seem to have been as important to him as his growing religious ones. His delight in medieval churches (and in the Gothic revival in architecture of William Butterfield, then working in Oxford, and his pupils) was closely bound up with Ruskin's admiration for medieval art; he read Ruskin's *Modern Painters* and entered the names of the Pre-Raphaelite Brotherhood in his diary; he became extremely interested in the contemporary schools of painting. His most ambitious undergraduate essay, *On the Origin of Beauty: a Platonic Dialogue*, seems clearly influenced by the chief spokesman of the aesthetic movement, Walter Pater, a Fellow of Brasenose since 1864. He later became a pupil of Pater's, and a book of his essays for him survives.

But even to a moderate Anglican, Pater's doctrine of 'art for art's sake' could never be satisfactory: and Hopkins's religion was never moderate. He went up to Oxford a convinced High Anglican and was soon a devoted follower of the Oxford High Church party's acknowledged leader Dr. Pusey and of his disciple, Canon Liddon. His closest friends (except Baillie, a free-thinker) were almost all High Churchmen—and several later went over to Rome; even Robert Bridges had thought of taking orders. Indeed it seems to have been his meeting with a school-friend of Bridges, the young poet and religious enthusiast Digby Mackworth Dolben,[1] that precipitated what was clearly a religious crisis in March 1865: a crisis which led to his diary entry of 12 March, 'A day

---

[1] Dolben was drowned, aged 19, in June 1867, while awaiting reception as a Roman Catholic. Bridges edited his poems, with a memoir, in 1911. Hopkins's sonnet, *Where art thou friend, whom I shall never see* (p. 39) was probably addressed to him.

of the great mercy of God', his first recorded confession two weeks later, and the keeping of daily notes—of extreme scrupulousness—for confession.

There can be no doubt that Hopkins now went through an intense struggle between opposing sides of his nature; and that a strong ascetic strain was predominant. On 6 November 1865 he recorded in his diary: 'On this day by God's grace I resolved to give up all beauty until I had His leave for it.' His Lent resolutions for 1866 (p. 114) include 'No verses in Passion Week or on Fridays'. The most striking of the poems he wrote at Oxford, *Heaven–Haven* (p. 38), *The Alchemist in the City* (p. 39), and *The Habit of Perfection* (p. 41), all suggest this struggle directly or implicitly.

His conversion to Rome came in July 1866, when he was on a Long Vacation reading-party in Sussex, and is recorded with characteristic exactness: 'July 17. . . .—It was this night I believe but possibly the next that I saw clearly the impossibility of staying in the Church of England.' But, as he later wrote to a friend, 'the silent conviction that I was to become a Catholic has been present to me for a year perhaps'. When he broke the news that October to his parents, to Liddon, and to Pusey, and faced first their desperate attempts to stop him and then their pain, he insisted that he claimed no 'personal illumination', but had worked out his position with irrevocable logic. The reasons for his conversion which he gave to his father have, indeed, most affinity with Newman's; and it was Newman whom he asked to receive him into the Roman Catholic Church that same month.

He remained at Oxford and the following summer added a First in 'Greats' to his First in 'Mods'. For two terms he taught for Newman at the Oratory School, Birmingham. Then in May 1868 he made three momentous decisions: to become a priest; to become a Jesuit ('Don't call "the Jesuit discipline"

hard; it will bring you to heaven', wrote Newman); and to
burn his poems. 'May 11. . . . Slaughter of the innocents' is
his laconic Journal entry; and Humphry House has argued
compellingly[1] that this must be the destruction to which
Hopkins referred ten years later in his famous letter to Canon
Dixon (p. 158).

The Romantic poets—and, even more, the Pre-Raphaelites
—had dedicated themselves to poetry as a religion. For seven
years Hopkins regarded it as incompatible with his vocation
as a priest. It was his own view, not that of his superiors, as
he later made clear to Bridges. And what he wrote to Baillie
this same year, 1868, about his painting may explain something of the rigorousness of his decision: 'You know I once
wanted to be a painter. But even if I could I would not I think,
now, for the fact is that the higher and more attractive parts
of the art put a strain upon the passions which I should think it
unsafe to encounter.' Both poetry and painting, in their very
appeal to the higher passions, might lure him away from
the single-minded election of a way of life laid down in the
Spiritual Exercises of St. Ignatius Loyola, the founder of the
Society of Jesus.

Instead, Hopkins' remarkable powers of observation, his
searching for distinctive beauty, for significant detail or
pattern in the natural world, find their outlet in his Journal
(which, again, includes many small sketches). For this beauty
of pattern which expresses a thing's inner form he coined the
word 'inscape'; and for the intense feeling it exerted on him,
the word 'instress'. 'Inscape' is first used, in the Journal, of
Swiss trees, on a Continental walking-tour of July 1868;
'instress', of the beauty of Giotto, inspired by a visit to the
National Gallery shortly before. Thereafter, both words occur
numerous times, to describe for himself the beauty and

[1] In *Journals and Papers*, Oxford, 1959, pp. 537–9.

impact of a multitude of objects. Trees, flowers, the sky, clouds, stars, glaciers, buildings, pictures, all have their own inscapes. 'All the world is full of inscape', he writes in one entry; and, in another, after admiring the beams of a great barn: 'I thought how sadly beauty of inscape was unknown and buried away from simple people and yet how near at hand it was if they had eyes to see it and it could be called out everywhere again.'

In a letter to Bridges he applied it to his own poetry: 'No doubt my poetry errs on the side of oddness. I hope in time to have a more balanced and Miltonic style. But as air, melody, is what strikes me most of all in music and design in painting, so design, pattern, or what I am in the habit of calling "inscape" is what I above all aim at in poetry. Now it is the virtue of design, pattern, or inscape to be distinctive and it is the vice of distinctiveness to become queer. This vice I cannot have escaped.' (15 February 1879)

The Journal anticipates Hopkins's mature poems in many other ways. In its excited, hypersensitive response to nature, it is full of 'wildness and wet', of 'the dearest freshness deep down things'. Unusual and strangely precise words are searched out—and sometimes coined—to express the inscapes he delighted in: 'dimpled . . . and . . . wimpled' (of leaves), 'sprigged, fretted' (of a waterfall), 'brindled and hatched, knopped, pelleted, ruddled' (of clouds), 'moulded in flutings, oyster-shell, pied' (of the sky). Both the sound and the look of the words are already working in ways in which more complex words will work in the poems.

On 7 September 1868 Hopkins entered the Jesuit Novitiate at Roehampton, near London, and began nine years' training and strict spiritual discipline for the priesthood. After two years he took his first vows of poverty, chastity, and obedience; he then studied philosophy at Stonyhurst, in

Lancashire; returned to Roehampton to teach 'rhetoric' for a year; and from 1874 studied theology at St. Beuno's College — 'pastoral forehead of Wales' of *The Wreck of the Deutschland*. On 23 September 1877 he was ordained. Every year of this training (and every year of his life as a Jesuit) he went through the *Spiritual Exercises* of St. Ignatius. In four weeks' meditations, the *Exercises* help the Jesuit to attain his goal of salvation: the ordering of his life, as a whole and daily, according to God's will for him. Hopkins's most important spiritual writing is the beginning of a Commentary on the *Exercises* (see pp. 144-5). They were central to his inner life, as they are to the life of every Jesuit. They had a profound effect on his poetry, as the sections of this Introduction on *The Wreck of the Deutschland* and the 1887-8 sonnets attempt to show (pp. 20-22).

When he became a Jesuit, Hopkins regarded the writing of poetry as 'unprofessional': two years before his ordination he wrote one of the greatest religious poems in the language. Many critics have insisted on a conflict between the strict discipline of his Jesuit training and his desire to create, to write poetry. There were certainly conflicts later in his life; and they were probably inevitable in a nature so fine as Hopkins's, so stern to itself, so prepared to suffer. Yet much of the evidence for the years that led to his priesthood points the other way.

Both his Journal and his later notes on the *Spiritual Exercises* show that he gradually saw his intense feeling for natural beauty—and, with it, his theory of inscape and instress—as a way to approach the supreme duty of his calling: to praise God through all created things. 'I do not think I have ever seen anything more beautiful than the bluebell I have been looking at', he wrote in 1870. 'I know the beauty of our Lord by it. Its inscape is mixed of strength and grace.' Two years later he found what seemed to be corroboration of his theories in the works of the thirteenth-century Franciscan philosopher, Duns Scotus, which he came across in the Stonyhurst library. He was, he said, 'flush with a new stroke of enthusiasm. It may come to nothing or it may be a mercy from God. But just then when I took in any inscape of the sky or sea I thought of Scotus' (p. 135).

Of the medieval theologians Duns Scotus put much the most stress on individuality, both of persons and things. He taught that the mind can apprehend the individual, concrete object, and through intuition of its 'this-ness' (*haecceitas*) finally come to know the universal; that such experiences of individual beauty ultimately reveal God; and that through directing such experiences towards God man can perfect his own especial *haecceitas*, his will. In all this Hopkins found support for his theory of inscape, and above all a religious sanction for it. Small wonder that a number of his poems show Scotus's influence and that one, *Duns Scotus's Oxford* (1879; p. 73), is devoted to his love for him 'who of all men most sways my spirits to peace; / Of realty the rarest-veinèd unraveller'. Scotus too lies behind much of his passage on the opening of the *Spiritual Exercises* (pp. 144–5), with its great paean to selfhood, 'this unspeakable stress of pitch, distinctiveness, and selving, this selfbeing of my own'. But the central inspiration of the *Exercises* for him was, as he put it in his notes, 'the great sacrifice': Christ's Passion and Crucifixion, which must be relived in His service. This paradox—the double awareness of the miracle of selfhood and the necessity of sacrifice—is faced in his first mature poem, *The Wreck of the Deutschland* (Winter, 1875–6). The conviction that he could at last devote such a poem to the glory of God is surely sufficient reason for the breaking of his seven years' silence.

But there were other reasons too for the revival of his poetic interests. During his year of teaching rhetoric at Roehampton (1873–4) he lectured on 'Rhythm and the other structural parts of Rhetoric—verse' (his lecture-notes survive); a short fragment 'Poetry and verse' is probably part of the same course. Again, the hope that he might once more write poetry was probably strengthened on his discovering, in January 1874, that his friend Bridges had just published a volume of poems. In a letter to him—the first for two and a half years—he said he was learning the piano, 'not for execution's sake but to be independent of others and learn something about music'. And—perhaps a final spur—on being sent to St. Beuno's that autumn he began to learn Welsh and to read Welsh poetry. In his letter to Canon Dixon of 5 October 1878 (p. 158), explaining how *The Deutschland* came to be written, he says: 'I had long had haunting my ear the echo of a new rhythm which now I realized on paper'; and he mentions 'certain chimes suggested by the Welsh poetry I had been reading (what they call *cynghanedd*)'. It is clear that a great many things came together when he was so moved by the account of the wreck of the *Deutschland*, and the Rector of St. Beuno's told him 'he wished someone would write a poem on the subject'. Wales ('always to me a mother of Muses') was in fact peculiarly fruitful for Hopkins's poetry: and in the year of his ordination he wrote ten of his most exuberant, inscape-filled poems.

After his ordination Hopkins suffered the first of what Fr. Christopher Devlin[1] has called his 'three wounds' in his expectation of a full and useful life in religion: he was not promoted to a further year of theological studies, as he had hoped to be. Instead, he served for the next four years as a priest in a succession of missions: in London, Chesterfield,

---

[1] *Sermons and Devotional Writings*, Oxford, 1959, Introduction, p. xiii.

Oxford, Bedford Leigh (near Manchester), Liverpool, and Glasgow. He entered on his duties with ardour, but he suffered from ill-health, and he was appalled by the moral and physical conditions of the northern industrial slums. Excusing himself to Bridges for not writing from Liverpool, he burst out in one letter: 'But I never could write; time and spirits were wanting; one is so fagged, so harried and gallied up and down. And the drunkards go on drinking, the filthy, as the scripture says, are filthy still: human nature is inveterate. Would that I had seen the last of it.'[1] But this was written in a fit of despair; several of the poems he wrote during this period—poems inspired by his experiences as a priest—show how strongly he could he moved still by human (and particularly youthful) nature:

> Ah Nature, framed in fault,
> There's comfort then, there's salt;
> Nature, bad, base, and blind,
> Dearly thou canst be kind. . . .
> (*Brothers*, 1880)

As a preacher Hopkins was not particularly successful. His sermons are utterly sincere; they are original and dramatic in ways that remind us of his poems; one of them, on the beauty of Christ, has a candour and poignancy peculiarly his own. But neither his voice nor his delivery seem to have been very effective; he was, he says, at times nervous and confused; and his originality was sometimes too much for his congregation. In one sermon he compared the Church filled with sacramental grace to a cow with full udders; his use of the word 'sweetheart' in another upset his Rector.

After eighteen wearying months in Liverpool (Bridges wrote that 'the vice and horrors nearly killed him'), and two

---

[1] 26 October 1880.

months in Glasgow, Hopkins was badly in need of the 'tertianship' (the third year of probation as a Jesuit), now due to him. He spent it at Roehampton. It was a time of spiritual renewal and mental refreshment, as several of his letters show. 'My mind', he wrote to Dixon, 'is here more at peace than it has ever been and I would gladly live all my life, it it were so to be, in as great or a greater seclusion from the world and be busied only with God.' He ended it too with a new confidence in his literary powers: he had begun his commentary on the *Exercises*; he had plans for a 'great ode' on the Jesuit martyr Edmund Campion and a verse play on St. Winefred, the Welsh saint, as well as for two prose works —on the idea of sacrifice and on Greek lyric art. Fragments of *St. Winefred* survive, including the Maidens' song, *The Leaden Echo and the Golden Echo;* the rest, sadly, were among the 'beginnings of things . . . ruins and wrecks', as he later called them to Baillie. One fine and important poem he did write, however, soon after the end of his tertianship: the sonnet that sums up much of his Scotist thought, '*As kingfishers catch fire*', in which the wonder of each thing expressing its own selfhood culminates in man, through grace, reaching the perfection of Christ.

From the end of his tertianship in 1882 until his death in 1889 Hopkins taught Classics: for two years to the Jesuit 'philosophers' at Stonyhurst, from 1884 at University College, Dublin—then under the control of the Jesuits—where he held the Chair of Greek and a Fellowship of the Royal University. These were intended to be congenial appointments for a natural scholar: the Provincial, in appointing him to Stonyhurst, had encouraged him to continue his writing. Yet his new confidence ebbed rapidly away. In March 1883 he wrote to Bridges: 'I am always jaded, I cannot tell why, and my vein shews no sign of ever flowing again'; and in

June to Dixon: 'I see no grounded prospect of my ever doing much not only in poetry but in anything at all. At times I do feel this sadly and bitterly, but it is God's will. . . .'. These were only the prelude to much more despairing cries from Dublin. His health seemed to be breaking up altogether; the frequent examining he had to do for the University played havoc with his eyes; he wrote to Bridges of 'recovering from a deep fit of nervous prostration'; to Baillie of his constitutional melancholy becoming 'more distributed, constant, and crippling'. He disapproved of Irish nationalism and of Gladstone's policy to give Ireland Home Rule; yet felt torn in his allegiance by some of the Catholic bishops' supporting it. Worst of all, he felt that his creative powers were utterly dead: in September 1885, the year of his lowest ebb, he wrote to Bridges, 'if I could but produce work I should not mind its being buried, silenced, and going no further; but it kills me to be time's eunuch and never to beget'. Yet in the same letter he promised him some sonnets, four of which 'came like inspirations unbidden and against my will': they are among six sonnets of desolation, probably all written that year, which as a group can claim to be his finest poems.

   Attempts to explain Hopkins's sense of desolation in Dublin have differed widely. Several critics have seen these four years as the climax to a conflict, conscious or unconscious, between the priest and the poet; and Hopkins, in his misery, as the victim of frustrated creative impulses. Catholic writers, at the other extreme, have shown that 'spiritual desolation' or 'aridity' is a state fully understood and prepared for in the *Spiritual Exercises*: to them Hopkins's experience of it was part of his predestined suffering in his search to identify himself with Christ's sacrifice. Others have seen in the self-torment of the sonnets an experience similar to that described by St. John of the Cross as the 'Dark Night of the Soul', and have claimed Hopkins as a mystical poet. Yet, for the true mystic, such suffering leads always to the sense of union with God; and, as Dr. Pick has pointed out,[1] nothing in Hopkins's poetry bears this interpretation. But, however harsh the internal struggle, nowhere in these sonnets does Hopkins deny God or His all-importance to him. He had written with truth to Dixon in 1881 that he had never wavered in his vocation; just as he had told Baillie, in an unforgettable phrase, ten years earlier, 'this life here though it is hard is God's will for me as I most intimately know, which is more than violets knee-deep' (10 April 1871).

Obviously, many factors played their part: his bad health, the drudgery of examining, his dislike of the political situation. But Fr. Devlin's seems to be the truest explanation of Hopkins's self-torment:[2] that, in his search for personal sanctity, he exaggerated the distinction between nature and duty—in theological terms, between his 'affective will', to which he assigned his love of beauty (including poetic beauty), and his 'elective will', to which he assigned his desire for holiness. Signs of this struggle are evident in almost all his surviving Retreat Notes. It explains the burning of his early verse, and his refusal to let Dixon publish one of his poems in 1879; it partly explains, too, his scruples about making his poetry known. In thus turning round on his poetic genius and treating it as a dangerous weakness, he behaved, as Fr. Devlin puts it, 'as a Victorian husband might to a wife of whom he had cause to be ashamed'.

A final point must be made. Hopkins was not intellectually isolated in either Stonyhurst or Dublin. He had congenial colleagues in both posts, and in Dublin he saw much of Fr.

[1] G. M. Hopkins: Priest and Poet, Oxford, 1942, p. 131.
[2] Sermons and Devotional Writings, Oxford, 1959, pp. 119–21, 218–21.

Matthew Russell, editor of the *Irish Monthly*, through whom
he met W. B. Yeats's father, the artist John Butler Yeats, and
the poet Katharine Tynan. He was carrying on long corres-
pondences with Bridges, Canon Dixon and, since 1883, with
Coventry Patmore: mainly giving them detailed and brilliant
criticism of their own poems, but occasionally still discussing
his own. He had new enthusiasms in music and, from 1886, in
Greek-Egyptian derivations of words, which he discussed in
long letters to Baillie. During the last year of his life he wrote
two poems very different from the sonnets of 1885: *That
Nature is a Heraclitean Fire and of the comfort of the Resurrection*,
which ends with the triumph and vindication of man, in all
his weakness, as 'immortal diamond'; and the delightful—
though unfinished—*Epithalamion*, to celebrate his brother's
marriage. It would be quite untrue to say that, even during his
Dublin years, he was perpetually despondent.

At the same time he did not receive the encouragement he
needed as a poet; and how much he needed it he knew well:
'There is a point with me in matters of any size when I must
absolutely have encouragement as much as crops rain; afterwards I am independent', he wrote to Bridges. Of the three
poets who saw his poems, Bridges was his only critic, indeed
his only true audience; but Hopkins's letters show how far he
failed to convert him to his experiments. Bridges kept the
manuscripts of his poems, he discussed their prosody in detail,
but he encouraged him in only a few: he remained on the
whole poetically incomprehending as well as antipathetic to
Hopkins's religion. It makes their devoted friendship all the
more remarkable. Canon Dixon responded to the poems
Hopkins sent him with 'delight, astonishment, & admiration';
he used the often-quoted phrase 'the terrible crystal'[1] of them;

[1] Taken from Ezek. I, xxii, as pointed out by Mrs. E. Duncan-Jones in
Notes & Queries, June 1956.

but his letters show no detailed understanding of Hopkins's wholly new poetic technique. Coventry Patmore, who fervently admired Hopkins as a man, had to confess his bewilderment with the poet: 'to me', he wrote to Bridges, 'his poetry has the effect of veins of pure gold embedded in masses of impracticable quartz'.

The Jesuits rejected both *The Deutschland* and *The Eurydice*; and, though Hopkins regarded lack of publication as part of his personal sacrifice, he well knew its value: 'fame,' he told Bridges, 'the being known, though in itself one of the most dangerous things to man, is nevertheless the true and appointed air, element, and setting of genius and its works'.

At the end of April 1889 Hopkins contracted typhoid fever, and on 8 June he died, seven weeks before his forty-fifth birthday. In a retreat in 1883 he had noted: 'today I earnestly asked our Lord to watch over my compositions . . . that he should have them as his own and employ or not employ them as he should see fit. And this I believe is heard.' To Dixon he wrote with equal humility, yet confidence, 'it may be that the time will come for my verses'. The time did come, but slowly. Bridges published a handful, from the manuscripts and copies he had scrupulously kept, in A. H. Miles's *Poets and Poetry of the Century*, 1893, and a few more in *The Spirit of Man*, 1915. In 1918 he published the first full edition, and the 750 copies took ten years to sell. It had taken forty years to establish Hopkins's reputation. Since then, his greatness has rarely been questioned.

II. THE POEMS

'Every true poet, I thought, must be original and originality a condition of poetic genius; so that each poet is like a species

in nature . . . and can never recur.' So Hopkins wrote to
Coventry Patmore in 1886; and to Bridges two years later:
'The effect of studying masterpieces is to make me admire
and do otherwise. So it must be on every original artist to
some degree, on me to a marked degree.' Hopkins was one
of our greatest original poets and, as his letters show, perfectly
conscious of the technical innovations he was making.
Bridges's charges in the Preface to his edition of his friend's
poems—of 'Oddity', 'Obscurity', ambiguities, false rhymes—
show how utterly inadequate it was (and is) to judge him by
the canons of normal Victorian poetic taste. He had an intense
need to bring together elements that in most of the poetry
of the previous two centuries—and certainly in the poetry
of his contemporaries—had been separated: absolute religious
conviction, extraordinarily sensitive feeling, a tough, realistic
intelligence.

His success in achieving this fusion was largely a matter of
using words, of employing their resources to the utmost, of
breaking down the conventional barriers between the spoken
language and 'the language of poetry'. He was quite explicit
about it to Bridges: 'it seems to me that the poetical language
of an age should be the current language heightened, to any
degree heightened and unlike itself, but not (I mean normally: passing freaks and graces are another thing) an obsolete
one. This is Shakespeare's and Milton's practice, and the
want of it will be fatal to Tennyson's Idylls and plays, to
Swinburne, and perhaps to Morris.' The insight into what was
lacking in his contemporaries is impressive (Hopkins is always
an impressive critic); the reference to Shakespeare gives the
clue to Hopkins's own peculiar strength. He might equally
well have named the practice of Donne or of George Herbert:
for Hopkins, in his mature poems, uses language as the
seventeenth-century Metaphysical poets used it. A bold

innovator as a Victorian, he was exploring back to the great age of English poetry. Few English poets—as his Diary notes and his letters show—have been so vitally aware of tradition.

His achievement becomes the more remarkable when we consider his early poems, written at school and at Oxford. The earliest show how readily his sensuousness absorbed the idiom of the young Keats: *A Vision of the Mermaids* (1862), for instance, exhibits an unusually strong fascination with colour:

> Plum-purple was the west; but spikes of light
> Spear'd open lustrous gashes, crimson-white;
> (Where the eye fix'd, fled the encrimsoning spot,
> And, gathering, floated where the gaze was not;)
> And through their parting lids there came and went
> Keen glimpses of the inner firmament. . . .

Four years later *The Habit of Perfection* expresses an equally keen desire for asceticism; yet the feeling for the senses to be denied is still predominantly Keatsian:

> Palate, the hutch of tasty lust,
> Desire not to be rinsed with wine:
> The can must be so sweet, the crust
> So fresh that comes in fasts divine!
> . . . .
> O feel-of-primrose hands, O feet
> That want the yield of plushy sward, . . .

That grasp on nature—or rather, the intimacy (the sense of something especially known) with which he expresses it—never deserts him: and in that sense only, it seems to me, is T. S. Eliot right to call him a 'nature poet'.[1] But his first, and in many ways his greatest, mature poem, *The Wreck of the Deutschland* (1875–6), shows how much too narrow

[1] *After Strange Gods*, London, 1934, p. 48.

is such a description. *The Deutschland* is at once a great technical achievement and a great—and deeply personal—religious poem; and it uses words, emblems, and images in ways strikingly reminiscent of much Metaphysical poetry. Many different strands in Hopkins's experience came together when he read the account of the shipwreck, as has been already said: the spiritual crisis of his own conversion and the experience of his seven years' poetic silence; his response to Duns Scotus; the 'new rhythm' he 'had long had haunting' his ear; the influence of the classical Welsh poetry he had been reading.

The two most impressive qualities of the poem are closely interrelated: its unity, that binds together the account of the shipwreck and Hopkins's own spiritual struggle and conversion; and the way in which the dramatic stress of the language reflects the stress of that struggle. As F. R. Leavis has well said, 'The wreck he describes is both occasion and symbol. He realizes it so vividly that he is in it; and it is at the same time in him.'[1] The poem's technical triumph serves the same purpose: both the new rhythm and the poetic devices that Hopkins uses to such great effect—alliteration, assonance, internal rhyming, and 'chiming' of consonants—combine to give it the maximum rhetorical emphasis and urgency.

The 'sprung' rhythm Hopkins here used for the first time has caused some difficulty; but this is largely because, to justify it—as well as the 'counterpointed' rhythm he used later—he wrote of both so elaborately in his Preface (printed by Bridges with the poems). In fact, his poems themselves are rhythmically their own magnificent vindication—especially when read aloud, as Hopkins continually insisted they should be. His explanation to Dixon of the sprung rhythm he had used in *The Deutschland* could hardly be simpler: 'To speak shortly, it consists in scanning by accents

[1] *New Bearings in English Poetry*, London, 1950, p. 176.

or stresses alone, without any account of the numbers of syllables, so that a foot may be one strong syllable or it may be many light and one strong.' It gave him, as he said, much greater flexibility and poetic effectiveness than the ordinary system.

In Part the First of *The Deutschland* the distribution of stresses in each stanza is 2–3–4–3–5–5–4–6; the scanning of, for example, Stanza 3, plays a major part in forcing home to us the mixed terror and joy of the experience Hopkins describes:

> The frówn of his fáce
> Befóre me, the húrtle of héll
> Behínd, whére, where was a, whére was a pláce?
> I whírled out wíngs that spéll
> And fléd with a flíng of the héart to the héart of the Hóst.
> My heárt, but you were dóvewínged, Í can téll,
> Cárrier-witted, I am bóld to bóast,
> To flásh from the fláme to the fláme then, tówer from the gráce to the gráce.

Other devices likewise compel us to share the experience: the alliteration and assonance throughout, that link more than the words together; the repetition of 'where' in line 3 that spells out the terrified lostness; the image and sound of the poet's heart as a bird changing from panic-stricken flight to the comfort of the pigeon's homecoming and then, with a flash, to the soaring confidence of, perhaps, a towering hawk. This is essentially a dramatic skill and energy, and it reminds us of Donne—in *Holy Sonnets*, XIII, for example:

> What if this present were the worlds last night?
> Marke in my heart, O Soule, where thou dost dwell,
> The picture of Christ crucified, and tell
> Whether that countenance can thee affright, . . .

It fully justifies, too, Hopkins's defence of sprung rhythm as 'the nearest to the rhythm of prose', with the freedom that gives, in his letter to Bridges of 21 August 1877 (p. 155).

The Wreck of the Deutschland is far from a simple poem: to see the full links between the two Parts, between the vivid account of the shipwreck and of the tall nun's cry to Christ and Hopkins's own spiritual agony and conversion, needs understanding of and at least sympathy with the idea of sacrifice; the experiences it deals with are deeply personal and complex. But, precisely because of this, it is the nearest we have to Hopkins's spiritual autobiography for ten crucial years of his life; it even hints at the desolation that later overwhelms him in Dublin. All his technical brilliance is here, at full stretch; his extremest inscapes of feeling ('I did say yes / O at lightning and lashed rod'—'I kiss my hand / To the stars, lovely-asunder / Starlight, wafting him out of it'); some of his most daring and assured metaphysical images: 'But it rides time like riding a river' (of the Incarnation); the likening of man's acceptance of the Crucifixion to a sloe bursting in his mouth and flushing him, 'sour or sweet, / Brim, in a flash full!'

In the poems that followed Hopkins further explored his innovations of language and rhythm (to sprung rhythm he added counterpointed rhythm and 'outriding' feet)[1]; but many of the themes are anticipated in *The Deutschland*. The key to the most exultant of the 1877–8 sonnets, for instance, is Stanza 5, 'I kiss my hand / To the stars': the finding of God's mystery in the beauty of nature. Here Hopkins glories in his grasp of the created world, in its texture and colour and wildness, but gives it back, presents it explicitly, to Christ. These poems, with all their sensuous excitement, have thus something of the formal pattern of an early seventeenth-

[1] For his explanations of both, see p. 160.

century 'poem of meditation' (George Herbert springs immediately to mind): first, there is the experience itself, born of Hopkins's passion for the beauty of nature's minute detail and communicated with his astonishing force of language; then its deliberate setting within an eternal context that alone gives it meaning for him. Furthermore, Hopkins (like the seventeenth-century meditative poets) feels intensely that the poem he has written is something created to praise Christ: it is a new piece of creation, organized in minute particulars as are all His other works, with a pattern and inscape distinctly its own. And, in writing it, the poet has carried out in his own way the opening and vital exercise of the *Spiritual Exercises*: the 'Principle or Foundation', which begins 'Man was created to praise, reverence, and serve God our Lord, and by this means to save his soul'. *The Windhover*, the finest of these sonnets, is dedicated explicitly 'To Christ our Lord'.

The Starlight Night, written early in 1877, conforms exactly to this pattern. The octet gives us the star-world, evoking, through its imagery, other values besides its beauty: order ('bright boroughs', 'circle-citadels'); mystery ('The grey lawns cold . . .'); movement, of trees and doves. Line 8 beautifully modulates the tone:

> Ah well! it is all a purchase, all is a prize.

The sestet both reveals it as Christ's home and lays down the price for fully experiencing its beauty: 'Prayer, patience, alms, vows.' Meditation has led to a call for action.

This characteristic energy—meditation leading to spiritual movement and action—is the keynote of most of the poems of this period. In *Pied Beauty* all Hopkins's love of the "dappled" —symbol of the distinctive, of life's multitudinousness—is brought together, given poise and order in the last two lines:

He fathers-forth whose beauty is past change:
Praise him.

Hurrahing in Harvest—perhaps the most simply ecstatic of all his poems—ends with a remarkable image which transforms the moment of understanding into pure, physically felt, activity: when the beholder suddenly comprehends that Christ is the source of the world's beauty,

The heart rears wings bold and bolder
And hurls for him, O half hurls earth for him off under his feet.

It is difficult to believe that *The Windhover*—written a few months before *Hurrahing in Harvest*—should differ from it so utterly in meaning and intent as some critics have found. Technically, the octet is probably the most impressive thing Hopkins ever did: image and rhythm catch every movement of the soaring, gliding kestrel, and hold it perfectly. The sestet is much more difficult and has had many interpretations.[1] Some critics have seen in it a subconscious conflict between Hopkins the poet and Hopkins the priest; for others there is no conflict at all.

At one extreme it has been seen as the priest's cry of envy for the sensuous, imaginative life symbolized by the kestrel;[2] as a poem of inner friction, illustrating the ambiguity of indecision, where two incompatible ways of life are intensely desired and given simultaneous expression.[3] At the other extreme, Catholic critics, and especially fellow-Jesuits, have read it as 'a poetic restatement of the great meditation on the Kingdom of Christ in the *Spiritual Exercises* of St. Ignatius';[4]

[1] Two are given in the notes, p. 183; and a great many discussed by Raymond V. Schoder, S. J., in *Immortal Diamond*, ed. Norman Weyand, S.J., London, 1949, pp. 275–306.

[2] I. A. Richards, *The Dial*, September 1926.

[3] William Empson, *Seven Types of Ambiguity*, London, 1947, p. 226.

[4] R. V. Schoder, S. J., in *Immortal Diamond* (above).

as Hopkins's positive consecration of his service and sacrifice
to Christ's cause. Without doubt there is in the poem a sense
of struggle, of tension. But both its remarkable energy, and
its similarity in *pattern* to the other poems of this period, point
to a positive intent. Hopkins's aim, surely, was to make the
beauty and activity of the kestrel his own: even if his own
chief activity should be the life of sacrifice of the Jesuit. Full
awareness of that paradox accounts sufficiently for the tension.

In several poems of these years there is indeed a conflict, but
a quite conscious one: between the beauty of nature and man's
sin or ugliness. In *God's Grandeur* the contrast is simple,
Blake-like, anti-urban: between 'the dearest freshness deep
down things' and 'man's smudge', 'man's smell'. It is a theme
that recurs several times: in *The Sea and the Skylark*, where the
lark's pure song shames man's degeneracy in 'this shallow
and frail town'; in *Duns Scotus's Oxford*, where 'graceless
growth' has confounded 'Rural rural keeping'; in *Ribblesdale*,
where selfish industrialist man will spoil 'Thy lovely dale'.

A strong feeling for innocent beauty threatened by corruption is the keynote of the small group of poems directly
inspired by Hopkins's experiences as a priest: *The Bugler's
First Communion*, *The Handsome Heart*, and *Brothers*, all written
1879–80. The unfinished *On the Portrait of Two Beautiful
Young People*, written much later in Ireland, echoes the same
experience. Together with *Felix Randal* (1880)—his lament
over a dying blacksmith—they are virtually his only poems
involving relations with other people. They have thus a
special interest; but our critical response may vary widely.
No one can doubt Hopkins's ardour, or miss the force of his
prayers for these innocents of his flock.

> March, kind comrade, abreast him;
> Dress his days to a dexterous and starlight order.
> > (*The Bugler's First Communion*):

such a plea shows the seriousness of his personal concern. But what to many has seemed delicacy, sympathy, pathos, has seemed to others sentimentality. Details like the bugler boy's parenthood or his 'regimental red' may remind us of Coleridge's charge against Wordsworth of '*accidentality*', 'the insertion of accidental circumstances' into a poem (normally quite untypical of Hopkins); or, alternatively, bring home what it is easy to forget: that in some ways Hopkins was very much of his age. If we do find something poetically unsatisfactory in some of this group of poems, the reason is surely that, as Humphry House has stressed, 'all his most intense experience was solitary'.[1] Their framework seems too simple: we miss the tension of the more urgent, complex poems about himself.

The point comes home when we examine his second shipwreck poem, *The Loss of the Eurydice* (1878). It is much simpler than *The Deutschland*, but the description of the storm —the urgency of the language, stressed by the sprung rhythm —suggests a more than outward violence:

> A beetling baldbright cloud thorough England
> Riding: there did storms not mingle? and
> Hailropes hustle and grind their
> Heavengravel? wolfsnow, worlds of it, wind there?

After the narrative of the captain, the rescued Sydney Fletcher, and the drowned sailor ('strung by duty . . . strained to beauty'), comes the bold leap of thought (again we are reminded of the Metaphysicals) that makes the wreck an analogue of England's lapse from Rome.

> He was but one like thousands more.
> Day and night I deplore
> My people and born own nation,
> Fast foundering own generation.

[1] *All In Due Time*, London, 1955, p. 166.

The last part of the poem gathers up both wreck and lapse into Hopkins's own pain that men should die without salvation.

> But to Christ lord of thunder
> Crouch; lay knee by earth low under . . .

Such a prayer, in its intensity, shows how intimately Hopkins felt himself involved in this plea for God's Providence.

Two sonnets in particular show the strength that Hopkins's poetry gained from the influence of Duns Scotus: *Henry Purcell* and '*As kingfishers catch fire*'. Both explore and celebrate self-distinctiveness, and are closely related to the passages on selfhood in Hopkins's note on *The Principle or Foundation* (pp. 144–5). *Henry Purcell* is much the more difficult: we sense the struggle to find the exact analogue to 'the forgèd feature' of Purcell's music, the notes that utter his 'abrupt self'. Hopkins finds it in a characteristically daring image, whose meaning, obscure at first, suddenly 'explodes' (as he said poetic meaning should): the image of a great sea-bird which, opening his wings for flight, unawares shows us the markings on his plumage that stamp his species:

> . . . so some great stormfowl, whenever he has walked his while
> The thunder-purple seabeach, plumèd purple-of-thunder,

> If a wuthering of his palmy snow-pinions scatter a colossal smile
> Off him, but meaning motion fans fresh our wits with wonder.

So Purcell's music expresses more than his thought or feeling: it incidentally shows us the distinctive marks of his genius. More than that, it utters—as Hopkins puts it in his argument above the poem—'the very make and species of man as created both in him and in all men generally'. This movement from individual self-expression to fulfilment of man's ultimate purpose reaches its climax in '*As kingfishers catch fire*'. The sonnet begins with the 'selving' (the word is Hopkins's own)

CHS

of kingfishers, dragonflies, stones, bells: it ends with man's
selving, his becoming—through grace—Christ Himself:

> Acts in God's eye what in God's eye he is—
> Christ—for Christ plays in ten thousand places,
> Lovely in limbs, and lovely in eyes not his
> To the Father through the features of men's faces.

It is difficult to read Hopkins's poems of transience and loss
—*Binsey Poplars*, *Spring and Fall*, the first chorus of *The
Leaden Echo and the Golden Echo*—without remembering
the vivid enjoyment of these 'Scotist' sonnets: the clash does
much to explain their poignancy. In all of them, in a sense,

> Ten or twelve, only ten or twelve
> Strokes of havoc únselve
> The sweet especial scene. . . .
>   (*Binsey Poplars*)

Likewise, his vigour of personal conviction—poetically at
its most confident in '*As kingfishers catch fire*'—throws into
sharpest relief the despair of his later and greatest sonnets.
For these are essentially poems of 'unselving' too: only the
'especial scene' is now his own heart, and he wreaks the havoc
himself. Whatever the reasons for his desolation in Dublin
(see pp. 12–13), the form it took was the war within. The
most pervasive image in these sonnets is therefore of struggle:
the key to their intensity is the physical force with which the
words embodying it are charged. They are Hopkins's most
Shakespearean poems, in that they compel us, by dramatic
means, to share his intimate experience; and they are filled
with echoes of words and images from Shakespeare's
tragedies, and particularly from *King Lear*.[1]

Spelt from Sibyl's Leaves (1884–5) introduces them in date
and prophesies (as its title implies) their theme. Technically,

[1] See W. H. Gardner, *G. M. Hopkins*, London, 1944, I, pp. 175–9.

it stands quite apart: the length of its lines (Hopkins called it 'the longest sonnet ever written') contrasts with the austere bareness of the eight later sonnets. But it presents already an impressive enough parable of the internal struggle: 'self in self steepèd and pashed'—as night overwhelms day—warns us of its violence; the bitter ending—the felt presence of the rack where 'thoughts against thoughts in groans grind'— drives home to us its inevitability. Repetition and alliteration have rarely been used so relentlessly.

These and similar devices Hopkins uses to intensify the effect of his later sonnets. Yet 'devices' gives a wrong impression. We are much more aware of the human voice speaking, questioning, pleading. The words used are mostly everyday words; the language (as Hopkins claimed poetic language should be) is 'the current language heightened'. Each sonnet strips the experience it records down to its essentials; it is presented nakedly, without self-pity, with the bitter authenticity of time and place. *Carrion Comfort* not only recreates the struggle that has wrenched Hopkins apart; it gives that struggle its exact context:

> That night, that year
> Of now done darkness I wretch lay wrestling with (my God!) my God.

'*I wake and feel the fell of dark*' expresses the exact moment and pressure of Hopkins's acutest despair as he awakes in the night: the ambiguities of 'fell' (night as an animal's hide, as fierce, as having fallen) strengthen the sense of claustrophobia. 'With witness I speak this', in its bareness, is eloquent confirmation.

By aiming at this pitch of concentration—and omitting any word that does not contribute to it—Hopkins achieves a new and powerful rhetoric. Two examples should suggest its impressiveness. *'To seem the stranger lies my lot'* records a frustrated inability to create. Most of the sonnet states the situation simply, with a restrained grief. The full agony comes in the sestet:

> Only what word
> Wisest my heart breeds dark heaven's baffling ban
> Bars or hell's spell thwarts.

The clotted movement of the words exactly mirrors the feeling of baffled frustration.

There is the same kind of achievement in *'My own heart let me more have pity on'*. The feeling in the octet is here more complex: it combines a knowledge that his torment is self-caused with a conviction that there is no way out. The resultant bewilderment is perfectly caught in the image at ll. 5–8:

> I cast for comfort I can no more get
> By groping round my comfortless, than blind
> Eyes in their dark can day or thirst can find
> Thirst's all-in-all in all a world of wet.

The packed syntax presents initial difficulties: the mind has to take in that 'dark' is the state of 'my comfortless' world, just as it is of the blind man's blackness; and that 'thirst' itself seeks water, just as blindness seeks light. Yet, in making such efforts, the reader shares precisely in the experience Hopkins records.

Tom's Garland (1887) has the same concentration, but not the same urgent feeling behind it. It lacks the inevitability of the earlier group of sonnets, and, without that, the difficulties of syntax obtrude and confuse. Hopkins himself, explaining its meaning to the bewildered Bridges, confessed he thought it 'in point of execution very highly wrought, too much so, I am afraid'.

Hopkins's Dublin poems are not all desolate. *Harry Plough-man* has some of the difficulties of *Tom's Garland*, but there is no mistaking its delight in the beauty of physical action perfectly performed. The unfinished *Epithalamion* conjures up more carefree enjoyment:

> how the boys
> With dare and with downdolphinry and bellbright bodies huddling out,
> Are earthworld, airworld, waterworld thorough hurled, all by turn and turn about.

That Nature is a Heraclitean Fire and of the comfort of the Resurrection, written in the last year of Hopkins's life, returns to the exuberant sprung rhythm of his sonnets of ten years earlier. It is remarkable both in its vitality of movement and in a heightening of language unusual in his later poems. Its ultimate direction is assured and positive: it moves through nature's flux and death's blotting-out of man to the Resurrection, and it ends on a note of absolute affirmation:

> In a flash, at a trumpet crash,
> I am all at once what Christ is,/since he was what I am, and
> This Jack, joke, poor potsherd,/patch, matchwood, immortal diamond,
> Is immortal diamond.

Such hope is rare enough in these later poems. But Hopkins has still a reservoir of feeling for the natural world on which to draw—even though he uses it to strengthen by contrast the sense of his own sterility:

> See, banks and brakes
> Now, leavèd how thick! lacèd they are again
> With fretty chervil, look, and fresh wind shakes
> Them; birds build—but not I build; no, but strain,
> Time's eunuch, and not breed one work that wakes.
> Mine, O thou lord of life, send my roots rain.

The sad irony is that this bitter conviction of failure follows —indeed is part of—the series of his greatest poems. His last poem, the sonnet to Bridges, both laments and explains his flagging inspiration:

> O then if in my lagging lines you miss
> The roll, the rise, the carol, the creation,
> My winter world, that scarcely breathes that bliss
> Now, yields you, with some sighs, our explanation.

The bitterness of the previous sonnet has given way to an art that, in the last line, is almost onomatopoeic.[1] The poem's perfect control and technical skill—their achievement in those circumstances—are, in some measure, the truest tribute to both Hopkins's character and his genius.

[1] As remarked by Miss E. E. Phare in *The Poetry of G. M. Hopkins*, Cambridge, 1933, p. 28.

CHRONOLOGICAL TABLE
of Hopkins's Life

1844 Born at Stratford, Essex (28 July).

1852 Family moves to Oak Hill, Hampstead. At a day-school in Hampstead.

1854–63 Boarder at Highgate School.

1857 Tour through Belgium and the Rhineland with his father and brother.

1860 Wins school poetry prize with *The Escorial* (Easter). Tour through South Germany with his father.

1863 *Winter with the Gulf Stream* published in *Once a Week*, 14 February. Wins a Classical Exhibition to Balliol College, Oxford.

1863–7 At Balliol College. Meets Robert Bridges, Alexander Baillie, William Addis. Writes most of his early poetry; sketches a good deal.

1864 Takes a First in 'Mods'.

1865 Meets Digby Mackworth Dolben (February). Has religious crisis and begins his daily spiritual notes (March).

1866 Decides to leave Church of England (17 or 18 July). Received into the Roman Catholic Church by Newman (21 October).

1867 Takes a First in 'Greats' and graduates B.A. In Paris (July).

1867–8 Teaches at the Oratory School, Birmingham.

1868 Decides to become a priest and a Jesuit. Burns his early poems (11 May). Walking-tour in Switzerland with Edward Bond (July). Enters the Jesuit Novitiate, Roehampton (7 September).

1870–3 Studies Philosophy at St. Mary's Hall, Stonyhurst.

1873–4 Teaches 'Rhetoric' at Roehampton, including a course on 'Poetry and verse'.

1874–7 Studies Theology at St. Beuno's College, North Wales.

1875–6 Writes *The Wreck of the Deutschland* (December–January).

1877 Ordained priest (23 September).

1877–8 Sub-minister at Mount St. Mary's College, Chesterfield.

1878 Select Preacher at Farm Street Church, London (August). Correspondence with R. W. Dixon begins (June).

1878–9 Priest at St. Aloysius's Church, Oxford.

1879 On temporary staff at St. Joseph's, Bedford Leigh, near Manchester (October).

1880–1 Priest at St. Francis Xavier's, Liverpool.

1881 On temporary staff at St. Joseph's, Glasgow (August–October).

1881–2 'Tertianship' at Roehampton.

1882–4 Teaches Classics at St. Mary's Hall, Stonyhurst.

1883 Correspondence with Coventry Patmore begins (August). In Holland with his parents (August).

1884–9 Professor of Greek, University College, Dublin, and Fellow of the Royal University.

1889 Dies in Dublin of typhoid fever (8 June).

1893 Eleven of his poems (three of them extracts), published by Bridges in A. H. Miles's *Poets and Poetry of the Century*.

1915 Six of his poems (two of them extracts) published by Bridges in *The Spirit of Man*.

1918 *Poems of Gerard Manley Hopkins* published, edited by Bridges.

SELECT BIBLIOGRAPHY

I. EDITIONS OF HOPKINS'S WORKS

(a) *Poetry*

Poems, ed. Robert Bridges (Oxford, 1918); 2nd edn, rev. and enlarged, ed. Charles Williams, 1930; 3rd edn, rev. and enlarged, ed. W. H. Gardner, 1948; 4th edn, rev. and enlarged, ed. W. H. Gardner and N. H. Mackenzie, 1967.

(b) *Letters*

Letters of G. M. Hopkins to R. Bridges, ed. C. C. Abbott (Oxford, 1935).

Correspondence of G. M. Hopkins and R. W. Dixon, ed. C. C. Abbott (Oxford, 1935).

Further Letters of G. M. Hopkins, ed. C. C. Abbott (Oxford, 1938); 2nd edn, rev. and enlarged, 1956.

(c) *Journals and Spiritual Writings*

Note-Books and Papers, ed. Humphry House (Oxford, 1937); 2nd edn, rev. and enlarged, 1959, as

Journals and Papers, ed. Humphry House, completed by G. Storey; and *Sermons and Devotional Writings*, ed. Christopher Devlin, S.J.

(d) *Selections*

A Selection of Poems and Prose, ed. W. H. Gardner (London, 1953).

Selected Poems, ed. James Reeves (London, 1953).

A Hopkins Reader [Poems and Prose], ed. John Pick (London, 1953).

II. BIOGRAPHY AND CRITICISM

(a) *Books*

G. F. Lahey, S.J., *G. M. Hopkins* (Oxford, 1930).

E. E. Phare, *The Poetry of G. M. Hopkins* (Cambridge, 1933).

John Pick, *G. M. Hopkins: Priest and Poet* (Oxford, 1942).

E. Ruggles, *G. M. Hopkins* (New York, 1944; London, 1947).

The Kenyon Critics, *G. M. Hopkins* (New Haven, 1945).

W. A. M. Peters, S.J., *G. M. Hopkins: A Critical Essay towards the Understanding of his Poetry* (Oxford, 1948).

Immortal Diamond: Studies in G. M. Hopkins, ed. Norman Weyland, S.J. (London, 1949).

Geoffrey Grigson, 'G. M. Hopkins', in *Writers and their Work*, British Council pamphlet no. 59 (London, 1955).

W. H. Gardner, *G. M. Hopkins: A Study of Poetic Idiosyncrasy in Relation to Poetic Tradition*, 2 vols. (London, 1944, 1949; rev. edn, 1959).

D. A. Downes, *G. M. Hopkins: A Study of his Ignatian Spirit* (London, 1960).

(b) Articles and Essays

F. R. Leavis, *New Bearings in English Poetry* (London, 1932; 2nd edn, 1950). *The Common Pursuit* (London, 1952).

Essays in *New Verse*, No. 14, 1935.

David Daiches, *Poetry and the Modern World* (Chicago, 1940).

Humphry House, *All In Good Time* (London, 1955).

F. N. Lees, 'G. M. Hopkins', in *The Pelican Guide to English Literature*, vol. VI, ed. Boris Ford (London, 1958; rev. edn, 1964).

NOTE ON THE TEXT

The text and order of the poems are based on the 4th edn. of *The Poems of G. M. Hopkins*, ed. W. H. Gardner and N. H. Mackenzie (Oxford, 1967). That edition incorporates several important changes from earlier editions (particularly in the last stanza of *Morning, Midday, and Evening Sacrifice* and in *Brothers*), as well as many minor ones.

The text of the prose is based on that of the editions listed under I, (*b*) and (*c*), in the Select Bibliography. Hopkins's abbreviations have been lengthened throughout.

Hopkins's Preface to his poems and prosodic notes (given in *Poems*, above) have been omitted: the simpler explanations of his use of Sprung and Counterpointed Rhythm that he gave to Bridges and Dixon are printed instead (see pp. 154–5 and 159–60).

SELECTIONS FROM EARLY POEMS
(? 1862–6)

Winter with the Gulf Stream

The boughs, the boughs are bare enough
But earth has never felt the snow.
Frost-furred our ivies are and rough

With bills of rime the brambles shew.
The hoarse leaves crawl on hissing ground   5
Because the sighing wind is low.

But if the rain-blasts be unbound
And from dank feathers wring the drops
The clogged brook runs with chosing sound

Kneading the mounded mire that stops   10
His channel under clammy coats
Of foliage fallen in the copse.

A simple passage of weak notes
Is all the winter bird dare try.
The bugle moon by daylight floats   15

So glassy white about the sky,
So like a berg of hyaline,
And pencilled blue so daintily,

I never saw her so divine.
But through black branches, rarely drest   20
In scarves of silky shot and shine,

The webbed and the watery west
Where yonder crimson fireball sits
Looks laid for feasting and for rest.

I see long reefs of violets   25
In beryl-coloured fens so dim,
A gold-water Pactolus frets

Its brindled wharves and yellow brim,
The waxen colours weep and run,
And slendering to his burning rim   30

Into the flat blue mist the sun
Drops out and all our day is done.

Heaven-Haven

A nun takes the veil

I have desired to go
     Where springs not fail,
To fields where flies no sharp and sided hail
     And a few lilies blow.

And I have asked to be   5
     Where no storms come,
Where the green swell is in the havens dumb,
     And out of the swing of the sea.

'Where art thou friend . . . ?'

Where art thou friend, whom I shall never see,
Conceiving whom I must conceive amiss?
Or sunder'd from my sight in the age that is
Or far-off promise of a time to be:
Thou who canst best accept the certainty   5
That thou hadst borne proportion in my bliss,
That likest in me either that or this,—
Oh! even for the weakness of the plea
That I have taken to plead with,—if the sound
Of God's dear pleadings have as yet not moved thee,—   10
And for those virtues I in thee have found,
Who say that had I known I had approved thee,—
For these, make all the virtues to abound,—
No, but for Christ who hath foreknown and loved thee.

The Alchemist in the City

My window shows the travelling clouds,
Leaves spent, new seasons, alter'd sky,
The making and the melting crowds:
The whole world passes; I stand by.

They do not waste their meted hours,   5
But men and masters plan and build:
I see the crowning of their towers,
And happy promises fulfill'd.

And I—perhaps if my intent
Could count on prediluvian age,   10
The labours I should then have spent
Might so attain their heritage,

But now before the pot can glow
With not to be discover'd gold,
At length the bellows shall not blow,　　　15
The furnace shall at last be cold.

Yet it is now too late to heal
The incapable and cumbrous shame
Which makes me when with men I deal
More powerless than the blind or lame.　　　20

No, I should love the city less
Even than this my thankless lore;
But I desire the wilderness
Or weeded landslips of the shore.

I walk my breezy belvedere　　　25
To watch the low or levant sun,
I see the city pigeons veer,
I mark the tower swallows run

Between the tower-top and the ground
Below me in the bearing air;　　　30
Then find in the horizon-round
One spot and hunger to be there.

And then I hate the most that lore
That holds no promise of success;
Then sweetest seems the houseless shore,　　　35
Then free and kind the wilderness.

Or ancient mounds that cover bones,
Or rocks where rockdoves do repair
And trees of terebinth and stones
And silence and a gulf of air.　　　40

There on a long and squarèd height
After the sunset I would lie,
And dierce the yellow waxen light
With free long looking ere I die.

'Let me be to Thee as the circling bird'

Let me be to Thee as the circling bird,
Or bat with tender and air-crisping wings
That shapes in half-light his departing rings,
From both of whom a changeless note is heard.

I have found my music in a common word,   5
Trying each pleasurable throat that sings
And every praisèd sequence of sweet strings,
And know infallibly which I preferred.

The authentic cadence was discovered late
Which ends those only strains that I approve,   10
And other science all gone out of date
And minor sweetness scarce made mention of:
I have found the dominant of my range and state—
Love, O my God, to call Thee Love and Love.

The Habit of Perfection

Elected Silence, sing to me
And beat upon my whorlèd ear,
Pipe me to pastures still and be
The music that I care to hear.

Dhs

Shape nothing, lips; be lovely-dumb: 5
It is the shut, the curfew sent
From there where all surrenders come
Which only makes you eloquent.

Be shellèd, eyes, with double dark
And find the uncreated light: 10
This ruck and reel which you remark
Coils, keeps, and teases simple sight.

Palate, the hutch of tasty lust,
Desire not to be rinsed with wine:
Than can must be so sweet, the crust   15
So fresh that come in fasts divine!

Nostrils, your careless breath that spend
Upon the stir and keep of pride,
What relish shall the censers send
Along the sanctuary side!   20

O feel-of-primrose hands, O feet
That want the yield of plushy sward,
But you shall walk the golden street
And you unhouse and house the Lord.

And, Poverty, be thou the bride   25
And now the marriage feast begun,
And lily-coloured clothes provide
Your spouse not laboured-at nor spun.

POEMS
(1876−89)

The Wreck
of the Deutschland

To the
happy memory of five Franciscan nuns
exiles by the Falck Laws
drowned between midnight and morning of
Dec. 7th, 1875

PART THE FIRST

I

Thou mastering me
God! giver of breath and bread;
World's strand, sway of the sea;
Lord of living and dead;
Thou hast bound bones and veins in me, fastened me   5
flesh,
And after it almost unmade, what with dread,
Thy doing: and dost thou touch me afresh?
Over again I feel thy finger and find thee.

2

I did say yes
O at lightning and lashed rod;   10
Thou heardst me truer than tongue confess
Thy terror, O Christ, O God;
Thou knowest the walls, altar and hour and night:
The swoon of a heart that the sweep and the hurl of
thee trod
Hard down with a horror of height: 15
And the midriff astrain with leaning of, laced with fire of
stress.

3

The frown of his face
Before me, the hurtle of hell
Behind, where, where was a, where was a place?
I whirled out wings that spell   20
And fled with a fling of the heart to the heart of the
Host.
My heart, but you were dovewinged, I can tell,
Carrier-witted, I am bold to boast,
To flash from the flame to the flame then, tower from the
grace to the grace.

4

I am soft sift   25
In an hourglass—at the wall
Fast, but mined with a motion, a drift,
And it crowds and it combs to the fall;
I steady as a water in a well, to a poise, to a pane,
But roped with, always, all the way down from the   30
tall
Fells or flanks of the voel, a vein
Of the gospel proffer, a pressure, a principle, Christ's gift.

5

I kiss my hand
To the stars, lovely-asunder
Starlight, wafting him out of it; and   35
Glow, glory in thunder;
Kiss my hand to the dappled-with-damson west:
Since, tho' he is under the world's splendour and
wonder,
His mystery must be instressed, stressed;
For I greet him the days I meet him, and bless when I   40
understand.

6

Not out of his bliss
Springs the stress felt
Nor first from heaven (and few know this)
Swings the stroke dealt—
Stroke and a stress that stars and storms deliver,   45
That guilt is hushed by, hearts are flushed by and
melt—
But it rides time like riding a river
(And here the faithful waver, the faithless fable and miss).

7

It dates from day
Of his going in Galilee;   50
Warm-laid grave of a womb-life grey;
Manger, maiden's knee;
The dense and the driven Passion, and frightful sweat:
Thence the discharge of it, there its swelling to be,
Though felt before, though in high flood yet—   55
What none would have known of it, only the heart,
being hard at bay,

8

Is out with it! Oh,
We lash with the best or worst
Word last! How a lush-kept plush-capped sloe
Will, mouthed to flesh-burst,   60
Gush!—flush the man, the being with it, sour or
sweet,
Brim, in a flash, full!—Hither then, last or first,
To hero of Calvary, Christ's feet—
Never ask if meaning it, wanting it, warned of it—men go.

9

Be adored among men,   65
God, three-numberèd form;
Wring thy rebel, dogged in den,
Man's malice, with wrecking and storm.
Beyond saying sweet, past telling of tongue,
Thou art lightning and love, I found it, a winter and
warm;   70
Father and fondler of heart thou hast wrung:
Hast thy dark descending and most art merciful then.

10

With an anvil-ding
And with fire in him forge thy will
Or rather, rather then, stealing as Spring   75
Through him, melt him but master him still:
Whether at once, as once at a crash Paul,
Or as Austin, a lingering-out swéet skíll,
Make mercy in all of us, out of us all
Mastery, but be adored, but be adored King.   80

PART THE SECOND

11

'Some find me a sword; some
The flange and the rail; flame,
Fang, or flood' goes Death on drum,
And storms bugle his fame.
But wé dream we are rooted in earth—Dust!   85
Flesh falls within sight of us, we, though our flower
the same,
Wave with the meadow, forget that there must
The sour scythe cringe, and the blear share come.

12

On Saturday sailed from Bremen,
American-outward-bound,   90
Take settler and seamen, tell men with women,
Two hundred souls in the round—
O Father, not under thy feathers nor ever as guessing
The goal was a shoal, of a fourth the doom to be
drowned;
Yet did the dark side of the bay of thy blessing   95
Not vault them, the million of rounds of thy mercy not
reeve even them in?

13

Into the snows she sweeps,
Hurling the haven behind,
The Deutschland, on Sunday; and so the sky keeps,
For the infinite air is unkind,   100

And the sea flint-flake, black-backed in the regular
  blow,
Sitting Eastnortheast, in cursed quarter, the wind;
   Wiry and white-fiery and whirlwind-swivellèd
     snow
Spins to the widow-making unchilding unfathering deeps.

14

          She drove in the dark to leeward,   105
          She struck—not a reef or a rock
       But the combs of a smother of sand: night drew
         her
          Dead to the Kentish Knock;
     And she beat the bank down with her bows and the
       ride of her keel;
     The breakers rolled on her beam with ruinous shock; 110
          And canvas and compass, the whorl and the
            wheel
Idle for ever to waft her or wind her with, these she
  endured.

15

          Hope had grown grey hairs,
          Hope had mourning on,
       Trenched with tears, carved with cares,   115
          Hope was twelve hours gone;
     And frightful a nightfall folded rueful a day
     Nor rescue, only rocket and lightship, shone,
          And lives at last were washing away:
To the shrouds they took,—they shook in the hurling   120
  and horrible airs.

16

One stirred from the rigging to save
The wild woman-kind below,
With a rope's end round the man, handy and
brave—
He was pitched to his death at a blow,
For all his dreadnought breast and braids of thew: 125
They could tell him for hours, dandled the to and fro
Through the cobbled foam-fleece. What could he
do
With the burl of the fountains of air, buck and the flood of
the wave?

17

They fought with God's cold—
And they could not and fell to the deck   130
(Crushed them) or water (and drowned them)
or rolled
With the sea-romp over the wreck.
Night roared, with the heart-break hearing a heart-broke
rabble,
The woman's wailing, the crying of child without
check—
Till a lioness arose breasting the babble,   135
A prophetess towered in the tumult, a virginal tongue
told.

18

Ah, touched in your bower of bone,
Are you! turned for an exquisite smart,
Have you! make words break from me here all
alone,
Do you!—mother of being in me, heart.   140

O unteachably after evil, but uttering truth,
Why tears! is it? tears; such a melting, a madrigal
   start!
      Never-eldering revel and river of youth,
What can it be, this glee? the good you have there of
   your own?

19

Sister, a sister calling   145
A master, her master and mine!—
And the inboard seas run swirling and hawling;
The rash smart sloggering brine
Blinds her; but she that weather sees one thing, one;
Has one fetch in her: she rears herself to divine   150
Ears, and the call of the tall nun
To the men in the tops and the tackle rode over the
   storm's brawling.

20

She was first of a five and came
Of a coifèd sisterhood.
(O Deutschland, double a desperate name!   155
   O world wide of its good!
But Gertrude, lily, and Luther, are two of a town,
Christ's lily and beast of the waste wood:
From life's dawn it is drawn down,
Abel is Cain's brother and breasts they have sucked the 160
   same.)

21

Loathed for a love men knew in them,
Banned by the land of their birth,
Rhine refused them, Thames would ruin them;
Surf, snow, river and earth

Gnashed: but thou art above, thou Orion of light;   165
Thy unchancelling poising palms were weighing the
    worth,
        Thou martyr-master: in thy sight
Storm flakes were scroll-leaved flowers, lily showers—
    sweet heaven was astrew in them.

22

        Five! the finding and sake
        And cipher of suffering Christ.   170
    Mark, the mark is of man's make
        And the word of it Sacrificed.
    But he scores it in scarlet himself on his own
        bespoken,
    Before-time-taken, dearest prizèd and priced—
        Stigma, signal, cinquefoil token   175
For lettering of the lamb's fleece, ruddying of the rose-
    flake.

23

        Joy fall to thee, father Francis,
        Drawn to the Life that died;
    With the gnarls of the nails in thee, niche of the
        lance, his
            Lovescape crucified   180
    And seal of his seraph-arrival! and these thy
        daughters
    And five-livèd and leavèd favour and pride,
        Are sisterly sealed in wild waters,
To bathe in his fall-gold mercies, to breathe in his all-fire
    glances.

24

Away in the loveable west,   185
    On a pastoral forehead of Wales,
I was under a roof here, I was at rest,
    And they the prey of the gales;
She to the black-about air, to the breaker, the thickly
Falling flakes, to the throng that catches and quails   190
    Was calling 'O Christ, Christ, come quickly':
The cross to her she calls Christ to her, christens her
    wild-worst Best.

25

The majesty! what did she mean?
    Breathe, arch and original Breath.
Is it love in her of the being as her lover had   195
    been?
    Breathe, body of lovely Death.
They were else-minded then, altogether, the men
Woke thee with a *we are perishing* in the weather of
    Gennesareth.
    Or is it that she cried for the crown then,
The keener to come at the comfort for feeling the   200
    combating keen?

26

For how to the heart's cheering
    The down-dugged ground-hugged grey
Hovers off, the jay-blue heavens appearing
    Of pied and peeled May!
Blue-beating and hoary-glow height; or night, still   205
    higher,
With belled fire and the moth-soft Milky Way,
    What by your measure is the heaven of desire,
The treasure never eyesight got, nor was ever guessed
    what for the hearing?

27

No, but it was not these.
The jading and jar of the cart,   210
Time's tasking, it is fathers that asking for ease
Of the sodden-with-its-sorrowing heart,
Not danger, electrical horror; then further it finds
The appealing of the Passion is tenderer in prayer
apart:
Other, I gather, in measure her mind's   215
Burden, in wind's burly and beat of endragonèd seas.

28

But how shall I . . . make me room there:
Reach me a . . . Fancy, come faster—
Strike you the sight of it? look at it loom there,
Thing that she . . . There then! the Master, 220
Ipse, the only one, Christ, King, Head:
He was to cure the extremity where he had cast her;
Do, deal, lord it with living and dead;
Let him ride, her pride, in his triumph, despatch and
have done with his doom there.

29

Ah! there was a heart right!   225
There was single eye!
Read the unshapeable shock night
And knew the who and the why;
Wording it how but by him that present and past,
Heaven and earth are word of, worded by?—   230
The Simon Peter of a soul! to the blast
Tarpeïan-fast, but a blown beacon of light.

30

Jesu, heart's light,
Jesu, maid's son,
What was the feast followed the night   235
Thou hadst glory of this nun?—
Feast of the one woman without stain.
For so conceivèd, so to conceive thee is done;
But here was heart-throe, birth of a brain,
Word, that heard and kept thee and uttered thee outright.   240

31

Well, she has thee for the pain, for the
Patience; but pity of the rest of them!
Heart, go and bleed at a bitterer vein for the
Comfortless unconfessed of them—
No not uncomforted: lovely-felicitous Providence   245
Finger of a tender of, O of a feathery delicacy, the
breast of the
Maiden could obey so, be a bell to, ring of it, and
Startle the poor sheep back! is the shipwreck then a harvest,
does tempest carry the grain for thee?

32

I admire thee, master of the tides,   250
Of the Yore-flood, of the year's fall;
The recurb and the recovery of the gulf's sides,
The girth of it and the wharf of it and the
wall;
Stanching, quenching ocean of a motionable mind;
Ground of being, and granite of it: past all   255
Grasp God, throned behind
Death with a sovereignty that heeds but hides, bodes but
abides;

33

With a mercy that outrides
The all of water, an ark
For the listener; for the lingerer with a love   260
glides
Lower than death and the dark;
A vein for the visiting of the past-prayer, pent in
prison,
The-last-breath penitent spirits—the uttermost mark
Our passion-plungèd giant risen,
The Christ of the Father compassionate, fetched in the   265
storm of his strides.

34

Now burn, new born to the world,
Double-naturèd name,
The heaven-flung, heart-fleshed, maiden-furled
Miracle-in-Mary-of-flame,
Mid-numberèd he in three of the thunder-throne!   270
Not a dooms-day dazzle in his coming nor dark as
he came;
Kind, but royally reclaiming his own;
A released shower, let flash to the shire, not a lightning of
fire hard-hurled.

35

Dame, at our door
Drowned, and among our shoals,   275
Remember us in the roads, the heaven-haven of
the Reward:
Our King back, Oh, upon English souls!
Let him easter in us, be a dayspring to the dimness
of us, be a crimson-cresseted east,

More brightening her, rare-dear Britain, as his reign
  rolls,
    Pride, rose, prince, hero of us, high-priest,   280
Our hearts' charity's hearth's fire, our thoughts' chivalry's
  throng's Lord.

The Silver Jubilee

*to James First Bishop of Shrewsbury on the 25th Year
of his Episcopate July 28, 1876*

Though no high-hung bells or din
Of braggart bugles cry it in—
  What is sound? Nature's round
Makes the Silver Jubilee.

Five and twenty years have run   5
Since sacred fountains to the sun
  Sprang, that but now were shut,
Showering Silver Jubilee.

Feasts, when we shall fall asleep,
Shrewsbury may see others keep;   10
  None but you this her true,
This her Silver Jubilee.

Not today we need lament
Your wealth of life is some way spent:
  Toil has shed round your head   15
Silver but for Jubilee.

Then for her whose velvet vales
Should have pealed with welcome, Wales,
   Let the chime of a rhyme
Utter Silver Jubilee.   20

Penmaen Pool

For the Visitors' Book at the Inn

Who long for rest, who look for pleasure
Away from counter, court, or school
O where live well your lease of leisure
But here at, here at Penmaen Pool?

You'll dare the Alp? you'll dart the skiff?—   5
Each sport has here its tackle and tool:
Come, plant the staff by Cadair cliff;
Come, swing the sculls on Penmaen Pool.

What's yonder?—Grizzled Dyphwys dim:
The triple-hummocked Giant's Stool,   10
Hoar messmate, hobs and nobs with him
To halve the bowl of Penmaen Pool.

And all the landscape under survey,
At tranquil turns, by nature's rule,
Rides repeated topsyturvy   15
In frank, in fairy Penmaen Pool.

And Charles's Wain, the wondrous seven,
And sheep-flock clouds like worlds of wool,
For all they shine so, high in heaven,
Shew brighter shaken in Penmaen Pool.   20

EHS

The Mawddach, how she trips! though throttled
If floodtide teeming thrills her full,
And mazy sands all water-wattled
Waylay her at ebb, past Penmaen Pool.

But what's to see in stormy weather,   25
When grey showers gather and gusts are cool?
Why, raindrop-roundels looped together
That lace the face of Penmaen Pool.

Then even in weariest wintry hour
Of New Year's month or surly Yule   30
Furred snows, charged tuft above tuft, tower
From darksome darksome Penmaen Pool.

And ever, if bound here hardest home,
You've parlour-pastime left and (who'll
Not honour it?) ale like goldy foam   35
That frocks an oar in Penmaen Pool.

Then come who pine for peace or pleasure
Away from counter, court, or school,
Spend here your measure of time and treasure
And taste the treats of Penmaen Pool.   40

God's Grandeur

The world is charged with the grandeur of God.
  It will flame out, like shining from shook foil;
  It gathers to a greatness, like the ooze of oil
Crushed. Why do men then now not reck his rod?

Generations have trod, have trod, have trod;   5
    And all is seared with trade; bleared, smeared with toil;
    And wears man's smudge and shares man's smell: the
        soil
Is bare now, nor can foot feel, being shod.

And for all this, nature is never spent;
    There lives the dearest freshness deep down things;   10
And though the last lights off the black West went
    Oh, morning, at the brown brink eastward, springs—
Because the Holy Ghost over the bent
    World broods with warm breast and with ah! bright
        wings.

The Starlight Night

Look at the stars! look, look up at the skies!
    O look at all the fire-folk sitting in the air!
    The bright boroughs, the circle-citadels there!
Down in dim woods the diamond delves! the elves'-eyes!
The grey lawns cold where gold, where quickgold lies!   5
    Wind-beat whitebeam! airy abeles set on a flare!
    Flake-doves sent floating forth at a farmyard scare!
Ah well! it is all a purchase, all is a prize.

Buy then! bid then!—What?—Prayer, patience, alms,
    vows.
Look, look: a May-mess, like on orchard boughs!   10
    Look! March-bloom, like on mealed-with-yellow
        sallows!
These are indeed the barn; withindoors house
The shocks. This piece-bright paling shuts the spouse
    Christ home, Christ and his mother and all his hallows.

Spring

Nothing is so beautiful as Spring—
    When weeds, in wheels, shoot long and lovely and lush;
    Thrush's eggs look little low heavens, and thrush
Through the echoing timber does so rinse and wring
The ear, it strikes like lightnings to hear him sing;   5
    The glassy peartree leaves and blooms, they brush
    The descending blue; that blue is all in a rush
With richness; the racing lambs too have fair their fling.

What is all this juice and all this joy?
    A strain of the earth's sweet being in the beginning   10
In Eden garden.—Have, get, before it cloy,
    Before it cloud, Christ, lord, and sour with sinning,
Innocent mind and Mayday in girl and boy,
    Most, O maid's child, thy choice and worthy the
      winning.

In the Valley of the Elwy

I remember a house where all were good
    To me, God knows, deserving no such thing:
    Comforting smell breathed at very entering,
Fetched fresh, as I suppose, off some sweet wood.
That cordial air made those kind people a hood   5
    All over, as a bevy of eggs the mothering wing
    Will, or mild nights the new morsels of Spring:
Why, it seemed of course; seemed of right it should.

Lovely the woods, waters, meadows, combes, vales,
All the air things wear that build this world of Wales; 10
   Only the inmate does not correspond:
God, lover of souls, swaying considerate scales,
Complete thy creature dear O where it fails,
   Being mighty a master, being a father and fond.

The Sea and the Skylark

On ear and ear two noises too old to end
   Trench—right, the tide that ramps against the shore;
   With a flood or a fall, low lull-off or all roar,
Frequenting there while moon shall wear and wend.

Left hand, off land, I hear the lark ascend,   5
   His rash-fresh re-winded new-skeinèd score
   In crisps of curl off wild winch whirl, and pour
And pelt music, till none's to spill nor spend.

How these two shame this shallow and frail town!
   How ring right out our sordid turbid time,   10
Being pure! We, life's pride and cared-for crown,

   Have lost that cheer and charm of earth's past prime:
Our make and making break, are breaking, down
   To man's last dust, drain fast towards man's first slime.

The Windhover:

To Christ our Lord

I caught this morning morning's minion, king-
  dom of daylight's dauphin, dapple-dawn-drawn Falcon,
    in his riding
  Of the rolling level underneath him steady air, and
    striding
High there, how he rung upon the rein of a wimpling
  wing
In his ecstasy! then off, off forth on swing,
  As a skate's heel sweeps smooth on a bow-bend: the   5
    hurl and gliding
  Rebuffed the big wind. My heart in hiding
Stirred for a bird,—the achieve of, the mastery of the
  thing!

Brute beauty and valour and act, oh, air, pride, plume, here
  Buckle! AND the fire that breaks from thee then, a
    billion
Times told lovelier, more dangerous, O my chevalier!   10

  No wonder of it: shéer plód makes plough down sillion
Shine, and blue-bleak embers, ah my dear,
  Fall, gall themselves, and gash gold-vermilion.

Pied Beauty

Glory be to God for dappled things—
   For skies of couple-colour as a brinded cow;
    For rose-moles all in stipple upon trout that swim;
Fresh-firecoal chestnut-falls; finches' wings;
   Landscape plotted and pieced—fold, fallow, and plough; 5
    And áll trádes, their gear and tackle and trim.

All things counter, original, spare, strange;
   Whatever is fickle, freckled (who knows how?)
    With swift, slow; sweet, sour; adazzle, dim;
He fathers-forth whose beauty is past change: 10
              Praise him.

Hurrahing in Harvest

Summer ends now; now, barbarous in beauty, the stooks
   rise
   Around; up above, what wind-walks! what lovely
    behaviour
   Of silk-sack clouds! has wilder, wilful-wavier
Meal-drift moulded ever and melted across skies?

I walk, I lift up, I lift up heart, eyes,   5
   Down all that glory in the heavens to glean our Saviour;
   And, éyes, heárt, what looks, what lips yet gave you a
Rapturous love's greeting of realer, of rounder replies?

And the azurous hung hills are his world-wielding shoulder
   Majestic—as a stallion stalwart, very-violet-sweet!—   10
These things, these things were here and but the beholder
   Wanting; which two when they once meet,
The heart réars wíngs bold and bolder
   And hurls for him, O half hurls earth for him off under
his feet.

The Caged Skylark

As a dare-gale skylark scanted in a dull cage
   Man's mounting spirit in his bone-house, mean house,
      dwells—
   That bird beyond the remembering his free fells;
This in drudgery, day-labouring-out life's age.

Though aloft on turf or perch or poor low stage,   5
   Both sing sometímes the sweetest, sweetest spells,
   Yet both droop deadly sómetimes in their cells
Or wring their barriers in bursts of fear or rage.

Not that the sweet-fowl, song-fowl, needs no rest—
Why, hear him, hear him babble and drop down to his   10
nest,
   But his own nest, wild nest, no prison.

Man's spirit will be flesh-bound when found at best,
But uncumberèd: meadow-down is not distressed
   For a rainbow footing it nor he for his bónes rísen.

The Lantern Out of Doors

Sometimes a lantern moves along the night,
  That interests our eyes. And who goes there?
  I think; where from and bound, I wonder, where,
With, all down darkness wide, his wading light?

Men go by me whom either beauty bright   5
  In mould or mind or what not else makes rare:
  They rain against our much-thick and marsh air
Rich beams, till death or distance buys them quite.

Death or distance soon consumes them: wind
  What most I may eye after, be in at the end   10
I cannot, and out of sight is out of mind.

Christ minds; Christ's interest, what to avow or amend
  There, éyes them, heart wánts, care haúnts, foot
    fóllows kínd,
Their ránsom, théir rescue, ánd first, fást, last friénd.

The Loss of the Eurydice

Foundered March 24, 1878

The Eurydice—it concerned thee, O Lord:
Three hundred souls, O alas! on board,
  Some asleep unawakened, all un-
warned, eleven fathoms fallen

Where she foundered! One stroke
Felled and furled them, the hearts of oak!
    And flockbells off the aerial
Downs' forefalls beat to the burial.

For did she pride her, freighted fully, on
Bounden bales or a hoard of bullion?—   10
    Precious passing measure,
Lads and men her lade and treasure.

She had come from a cruise, training seamen—
Men, boldboys soon to be men:
    Must it, worst weather,   15
Blast bole and bloom together?

No Atlantic squall overwrought her
Or rearing billow of the Biscay water:
    Home was hard at hand
And the blow bore from land.   20

And you were a liar, O blue March day.
Bright sun lanced fire in the heavenly bay;
    But what black Boreas wrecked her? he
Came equipped, deadly-electric,

A beetling baldbright cloud thorough England   25
Riding: there did storms not mingle? and
    Hailropes hustle and grind their
Heavengravel? wolfsnow, worlds of it, wind there?

Now Carisbrook keep goes under in gloom;
Now it overvaults Appledurcombe;   30
    Now near by Ventnor town
It hurls, hurls off Boniface Down.

Too proud, too proud, what a press she bore!
Royal, and all her royals wore.
    Sharp with her, shorten sail! 35
Too late; lost; gone with the gale.

This was that fell capsize.
As half she had righted and hoped to rise
    Death teeming in by her portholes
Raced down decks, round messes of mortals. 40

Then a lurch forward, frigate and men;
'All hands for themselves' the cry ran then;
    But she who had housed them thither
Was around them, bound them or wound them with her.

Marcus Hare, high her captain, 45
Kept to her—care-drowned and wrapped in
    Cheer's death, would follow
His charge through the champ-white water-in-a-wallow,

All under Channel to bury in a beach her
Cheeks: Right, rude of feature, 50
    He thought he heard say
'Her commander! and thou too, and thou this way.'

It is even seen, time's something server,
In mankind's medley a duty-swerver,
    At downright 'No or Yes?' 55
Doffs all, drives full for righteousness.

Sydney Fletcher, Bristol-bred,
(Low lie his mates now on watery bed)
    Takes to the seas and snows
As sheer down the ship goes. 60

Now her afterdraught gullies him too down;
Now he wrings for breath with the deathgush brown;
   Till a lifebelt and God's will
Lend him a lift from the sea-swill.

Now he shoots short up to the round air;   65
Now he gasps, now he gazes everywhere;
   But his eye no cliff, no coast or
Mark makes in the rivelling snowstorm.

Him, after an hour of wintry waves,
A schooner sights, with another, and saves,   70
   And he boards her in Oh! such joy
He has lost count what came next, poor boy.—

They say who saw one sea-corpse cold
He was all of lovely manly mould,
   Every inch a tar,   75
Of the best we boast our sailors are.

Look, foot to forelock, how all things suit! he
Is strung by duty, is strained to beauty,
   And brown-as-dawning-skinned
With brine and shine and whirling wind.   80

O his nimble finger, his gnarled grip!
Leagues, leagues of seamanship
   Slumber in these forsaken
Bones, this sinew, and will not waken.

He was but one like thousands more.   85
Day and night I deplore
   My people and born own nation,
Fast foundering own generation.

I might let bygones be—our curse
Of ruinous shrine no hand or, worse,   90
    Robbery's hand is busy to
Dress, hoar-hallowèd shrines unvisited;

Only the breathing temple and fleet
Life, this wildworth blown so sweet,
    These daredeaths, ay this crew, in   95
Unchrist, all rolled in ruin—

Deeply surely I need to deplore it,
Wondering why my master bore it,
    The riving off that race
So at home, time was, to his truth and grace   100

That a starlight-wender of ours would say
The marvellous Milk was Walsingham Way
    And one—but let be, let be:
More, more than was will yet be.—

O well wept, mother have lost son;   105
Wept, wife; wept, sweetheart would be one:
    Though grief yield them no good
Yet shed what tears sad truelove should.

But to Christ lord of thunder
Crouch; lay knee by earth low under: 110
    'Holiest, loveliest, bravest,
Save my hero, O Hero savest.

And the prayer thou hearst me making
Have, at the awful overtaking,
    Heard; have heard and granted   115
Grace that day grace was wanted.'

Not that hell knows redeeming,
But for souls sunk in seeming
    Fresh, till doomfire burn all,
Prayer shall fetch pity eternal.   120

The May Magnificat

May is Mary's month, and I
Muse at that and wonder why:
    Her feasts follow reason,
    Dated due to season—

Candlemas, Lady Day;   5
But the Lady Month, May,
    Why fasten that upon her,
    With a feasting in her honour?

Is it only its being brighter
Than the most are must delight her?   10
    Is it opportunest
    And flowers finds soonest?

Ask of her, the mighty mother:
Her reply puts this other
    Question: What is Spring?—   15
    Growth in every thing—

Flesh and fleece, fur and feather,
Grass and greenworld all together;
    Star-eyed strawberry-breasted
    Throstle above her nested   20

Cluster of bugle blue eggs thin
Forms and warms the life within;
 And bird and blossom swell
 In sod or sheath or shell.

All things rising, all things sizing   25
Mary sees, sympathising
 With that world of good,
 Nature's motherhood.

Their magnifying of each its kind
With delight calls to mind   30
 How she did in her stored
 Magnify the Lord.

Well but there was more than this:
Spring's universal bliss
 Much, had much to say   35
 To offering Mary May.

When drop-of-blood-and-foam-dapple
Bloom lights the orchard-apple
 And thicket and thorp are merry
 With silver-surfèd cherry. 40

And azuring-over greybell makes
Wood banks and brakes wash wet like lakes
 And magic cuckoocall
 Caps, clears, and clinches all—

This ecstasy all through mothering earth 45
Tells Mary her mirth till Christ's birth
 To remember and exultation
 In God who was her salvation.

Binsey Poplars

felled 1879

My aspens dear, whose airy cages quelled,
Quelled or quenched in leaves the leaping sun,
All felled, felled, are all felled;
  Of a fresh and following folded rank
      Not spared, not one   5
      That dandled a sandalled
      Shadow that swam or sank
On meadow and river and wind-wandering weed-
  winding bank.

  O if we but knew what we do
      When we delve or hew—   10
    Hack and rack the growing green!
      Since country is so tender
    To touch, her being só slender,
    That, like this sleek and seeing ball
    But a prick will make no eye at all,   15
    Where we, even where we mean

      To mend her we end her,
      When we hew or delve:
After-comers cannot guess the beauty been.
  Ten or twelve, only ten or twelve   20
      Strokes of havoc únselve
      The sweet especial scene,
    Rural scene, a rural scene,
    Sweet especial rural scene.

Duns Scotus's Oxford

Towery city and branchy between towers;
Cuckoo-echoing, bell-swarmèd, lark-charmèd, rook-
    racked, river-rounded;
The dapple-eared lily below thee; that country and town
    did
Once encounter in, here coped and poisèd powers;

Thou hast a base and brickish skirt there, sours   5
That neighbour-nature thy grey beauty is grounded
Best in; graceless growth, thou hast confounded
Rural rural keeping—folk, flocks, and flowers.

Yet ah! this air I gather and I release
He lived on; these weeds and waters, these walls are what 10
He haunted who of all men most sways my spirits to peace;

Of realty the rarest-veinèd unraveller; a not
Rivalled insight, be rival Italy or Greece;
Who fired France for Mary without spot.

Henry Purcell

The poet wishes well to the divine genius of Purcell and praises him that, whereas other musicians have given utterance to the moods of man's mind, he has, beyond that, uttered in notes the very make and species of man as created both in him and in all men generally.

Have fair fallen, O fair, fair have fallen, so dear
To me, so arch-especial a spirit as heaves in Henry Purcell,
An age is now since passed, since parted; with the reversal
Of the outward sentence low lays him, listed to a heresy, here.

Not mood in him nor meaning, proud fire or sacred fear,   5
Or love, or pity, or all that sweet notes not his might
  nursle:
It is the forgèd feature finds me; it is the rehearsal
Of own, of abrúpt sélf there so thrusts on, so throngs the ear.

Let him oh! with his air of angels then lift me, lay me!
  only I'll
Have an eye to the sakes of him, quaint moonmarks, to   10
  his pelted plumage under
Wings: so some great stormfowl, whenever he has walked
  his while

The thunder-purple seabeach, plumèd purple-of-thunder,
If a wuthering of his palmy snow-pinions scatter a colossal
  smile
Off him, but meaning motion fans fresh our wits with
  wonder.

The Candle Indoors

Some candle clear burns somewhere I come by.
I muse at how its being puts blissful back
With yellowy moisture mild night's blear-all black,
Or to-fro tender trambeams truckle at the eye.
By that window what task what fingers ply,   5
I plod wondering, a-wanting, just for lack
Of answer the eagerer a-wanting Jessy or Jack
There/ God to aggrándise, God to glorify.—

Come you indoors, come home; your fading fire
Mend first and vital candle in close heart's vault: 10
You there are master, do your own desire;
What hinders? Are you beam-blind, yet to a fault
In a neighbour deft-handed? are you that liar
And, cast by conscience out, spendsavour salt?

The Handsome Heart:

at a Gracious Answer

'But tell me, child, your choice; what shall I buy
You?'—'Father, what you buy me I like best.'
With the sweetest air that said, still plied and pressed,
He swung to his first poised purport of reply.

What the heart is! which, like carriers let fly—   5
Doff darkness, homing nature knows the rest—
To its own fine function, wild and self-instressed,
Falls light as ten years long taught how to and why.

Mannerly-hearted! more than handsome face—
Beauty's bearing or muse of mounting vein,   10
All, in this case, bathed in high hallowing grace . . .

Of heaven what boon to buy you, boy, or gain
Not granted!—Only . . . O on that path you pace
Run all your race, O brace sterner that strain!

The Bugler's First Communion

A bugler boy from barrack (it is over the hill
There)—boy bugler, born, he tells me, of Irish
          Mother to an English sire (he
Shares their best gifts surely, fall how things will),

This very very day came down to us after a boon he on   5
My late being there begged of me, overflowing
          Boon in my bestowing,
Came, I say, this day to it—to a First Communion.

Here he knelt then ín regimental red.
Forth Christ from cupboard fetched, how fain I of feet   10
          To his youngster take his treat!
Low-latched in leaf-light housel his too huge godhead.

There! and your sweetest sendings, ah divine,
By it, heavens, befall him! as a heart Christ's darling,
          dauntless;
          Tongue true, vaunt- and tauntless;   15
Breathing bloom of a chastity in mansex fine.

Frowning and forefending angel-warder
Squander the hell-rook ranks sally to molest him;
    March, kind comrade, abreast him;
Dress his days to a dexterous and starlight order.   20

How it dóes my heart good, visiting at that bleak hill,
When limber liquid youth, that to all I teach
    Yields tender as a pushed peach,
Hies headstrong to its wellbeing of a self-wise self-will!

Then though I should tread tufts of consolation   25
Dáys áfter, só I in a sort deserve to
    And do serve God to serve to
Just such slips of soldiery Christ's royal ration.

Nothing élse is like it, no, not all so strains
Us: fresh youth fretted in a bloomfall all portending   30
    That sweet's sweeter ending;
Realm both Christ is heir to and thére réigns.

O now well work that sealing sacred ointment!
O for now charms, arms, what bans off bad
    And locks love ever in a lad!   35
Let mé though see no more of him, and not disappoint-
    ment

Those sweet hopes quell whose least me quickenings lift,
In scarlet or somewhere of some day seeing
    That brow and bead of being,
An our day's God's own Galahad. Though this child's   40
    drift

Seems by a divíne doom chánnelled, nor do I cry
Disaster there; but may he not rankle and roam
    In backwheels though bound home?—
That left to the Lord of the Eucharist, I here lie by;

Recorded only, I have put my lips on pleas   45
Would brandle adamantine heaven with ride and jar, did
    Prayer go disregarded:
Forward-like, but however, and like favourable heaven
  heard these.

Morning, Midday, and Evening Sacrifice

    The dappled die-away
    Cheek and the wimpled lip,
    The gold-wisp, the airy-grey
    Eye, all in fellowship—
    This, all this, beauty blooming,   5
    This, all this, freshness fuming,
    Give God while worth consuming.

    Both thought and thew now bolder
    And told by Nature: Tower;
    Head, heart, hand, heel, and shoulder   10
    That beat and breathe in power—

    This pride of prime's enjoyment
    Take as for tool, not toy meant
    And hold at Christ's employment.

The vault and scope and schooling   15
And mastery in the mind,
In silk-ash kept from cooling,
And ripest under rind—
What death half lifts the latch of,
What hell hopes soon the snatch of,   20
Your offering, with despatch, of!

Andromeda

Now Time's Andromeda on this rock rude,
With not her either beauty's equal or
Her injury's, looks off by both horns of shore,
Her flower, her piece of being, doomed dragon food.
   Time past she has been attempted and pursued   5
By many blows and banes; but now hears roar
A wilder beast from West than all were, more
Rife in her wrongs, more lawless, and more lewd.

   Her Perseus linger and leave her tó her extremes?—
Pillowy air he treads a time and hangs   10
His thoughts on her, forsaken that she seems,
   All while her patience, morselled into pangs,
Mounts; then to alight disarming, no one dreams,
With Gorgon's gear and barebill/ thongs and fangs.

Peace

When will you ever, Peace, wild wooddove, shy wings
   shut,
Your round me roaming end, and under be my boughs?
When, when, Peace, will you, Peace? I'll not play
   hypocrite
To own my heart: I yield you do come sometimes; but
That piecemeal peace is poor peace. What pure peace   5
   allows
Alarms of wars, the daunting wars, the death of it?

O surely, reaving Peace, my Lord should leave in lieu
Some good! And so he does leave Patience exquisite,
That plumes to Peace thereafter. And when Peace here
   does house
He comes with work to do, he does not come to coo,   10
       He comes to brood and sit.

At the Wedding March

God with honour hang your head,
Groom, and grace you, bride, your bed
With lissome scions, sweet scions,
Out of hallowed bodies bred.

Each be other's comfort kind: 5
Déep, déeper than divined,
Divine charity, dear charity,
Fast you ever, fast bind.

Then let the March tread our ears:
I to him turn with tears   10
Who to wedlock, his wonder wedlock,
Déals tríumph and immortal years.

Felix Randal

Felix Randal the farrier, O is he dead then? my duty all
  ended,
Who have watched his mould of man, big-boned and
  hardy-handsome
Pining, pining, till time when reason rambled in it and
  some
Fatal four disorders, fleshed there, all contended?

Sickness broke him. Impatient, he cursed at first, but   5
  mended
Being anointed and all; though a heavenlier heart began
  some
Months earlier, since I had our sweet reprieve and ransom
Tendered to him. Ah well, God rest him all road ever he
  offended!

This seeing the sick endears them to us, us too it endears.
My tongue had taught thee comfort, touch had quenched 10
  thy tears,
Thy tears that touched my heart, child, Felix, poor Felix
  Randal;

How far from then forethought of, all thy more boisterous
  years,
When thou at the random grim forge, powerful amidst
  peers,
Didst fettle for the great grey drayhorse his bright and
  battering sandal!

Brothers

How lovely the elder brother's
Life all laced in the other's,
Lóve-laced!—what once I well
Witnessed; so fortune fell.
When Shrovetide, two years gone,   5
Our boys' plays brought on
Part was picked for John,
Young Jóhn; then fear, then joy
Ran revel in the elder boy.
Now the night come; all   10
Our company thronged the hall;
Henry, by the wall,
Beckoned me beside him:
I came where called, and eyed him
By meanwhiles; making mý play   15
Turn most on tender byplay.
For, wrung all on love's rack,
My lad, and lost in Jack,
Smiled, blushed, and bit his lip;
Or drove, with a diver's dip,   20
Clutched hands through claspèd knees;
And many a mark like these,

Told tales with what heart's stress
He hung on the imp's success.
Now the other was bráss-bóld: 25
Hé had no work to hold
His heart up at the strain;
Nay, roguish ran the vein.
Two tedious acts were past;
Jack's call and cue at last;   30
When Henry, heart-forsook,
Dropped eyes and dared not look.
Thére! the háll rúng!
Dog, he did give tongue!
But Harry—in his hands he has flung   35
His tear-tricked cheeks of flame
For fond love and for shame.
   Ah Nature, framed in fault,
There's comfort then, there's salt;
Nature, bad, base, and blind,   40
Dearly thou canst be kind;
There dearly thén, deárly,
Dearly thou canst be kind.

Spring and Fall:

to a young child

Márgarét, áre you gríeving
Over Goldengrove unleaving?
Leáves líke the things of man, you
With your fresh thoughts care for, can you?
Ah! ás the heart grows older   5
It will come to such sights colder

By and by, nor spare a sigh
Though worlds of wanwood leafmeal lie;
And yet you *will* weep and know why.
Now no matter, child, the name: 10
Sórrow's spríngs áre the same.
Nor mouth had, no nor mind, expressed
What heart heard of, ghost guessed:
It ís the blight man was born for,
It is Margaret you mourn for.   15

Inversnaid

This darksome burn, horseback brown,
His rollrock highroad roaring down,
In coop and in comb the fleece of his foam
Flutes and low to the lake falls home.

A windpuff-bonnet of fáwn-fróth   5
Turns and twindles over the broth
Of a pool so pitchblack, féll-frówning,
It rounds and rounds Despair to drowning.

Degged with dew, dappled with dew
Are the groins of the braes that the brook treads through, 10
Wiry heathpacks, flitches of fern,
And the beadbonny ash that sits over the burn.

What would the world be, once bereft
Of wet and of wildness? Let them be left,
O let them be left, wildness and wet;   15
Long live the weeds and the wilderness yet.

'As kingfishers catch fire'

As kingfishers catch fire, dragonflies draw flame;
As tumbled over rim in roundy wells
Stones ring; like each tucked string tells, each hung bell's
Bow swung finds tongue to fling out broad its name;
Each mortal thing does one thing and the same: 5
Deals out that being indoors each one dwells;
Selves—goes itself; *myself* it speaks and spells,
Crying *What I do is me: for that I came.*

I say more: the just man justices;
Keeps gráce: thát keeps all his goings graces;   10
Acts in God's eye what in God's eye he is—
Chríst—for Christ plays in ten thousand places,
Lovely in limbs, and lovely in eyes not his
To the Father through the features of men's faces.

Ribblesdale

Earth, sweet Earth, sweet landscape, with leavès throng
And louchèd low grass, heaven that dost appeal
To, with no tongue to plead, no heart to feel;
That canst but only be, but dost that long—

Thou canst but be, but that thou well dost; strong   5
Thy plea with him who dealt, nay does now deal,
Thy lovely dale down thus and thus bids reel
Thy river, and o'er gives all to rack or wrong.

And what is Earth's eye, tongue, or heart else, where
Else, but in dear and dogged man?—Ah, the heir   10
To his own selfbent so bound, so tied to his turn,
To thriftless reave both our rich round world bare
And none reck of world after, this bids wear
Earth brows of such care, care and dear concern.

The Leaden Echo and the Golden Echo

(Maiden's song from St. Winefred's Well)

THE LEADEN ECHO

How to kéep—is there ány any, is there none such, nowhere
    known some, bow or brooch or braid or brace, láce,
    latch or catch or key to keep
Back beauty, keep it, beauty, beauty, beauty, . . . from
    vanishing away?
Ó is there no frowning of these wrinkles, rankèd wrinkles
    deep,
Dówn? no waving off of these most mournful messengers, still
    messengers, sad and stealing messengers of grey?—
No there's none, there's none, O no there's none,   5
Nor can you long be, what you now are, called fair,
Do what you may do, what, do what you may,
And wisdom is early to despair:
Be beginning; since, no, nothing can be done
To keep at bay   10
Age and age's evils, hoar hair,
Ruck and wrinkle, drooping, dying, death's worst,
    winding sheets, tombs and worms and tumbling to decay;
So be beginning, be beginning to despair.
O there's none; no no no there's none:
Be beginning to despair, to despair,   15
Despair, despair, despair, despair.

THE GOLDEN ECHO

Spare!
There ís one, yes I have one (Hush there!);
Only not within seeing of the sun.
Not within the singeing of the strong sun,
Tall sun's tingeing, or treacherous the tainting of the earth's
    air,   5
Somewhere elsewhere there is ah well where! one,
Óne. Yes I cán tell such a key, I dó know such a place,
Where whatever's prized and passes of us, everything that's
    fresh and fast flying of us, seems to us sweet of us and
    swiftly away with, done away with, undone,
Úndone, done with, soon done with, and yet dearly and
    dangerously sweet
Of us, the wimpled-water-dimpled, not-by-morning-   10
    matchèd face,
The flower of beauty, fleece of beauty, too too apt to,
    ah! to fleet,
Never fleets móre, fastened with the tenderest truth
To its own best being and its loveliness of youth: it is an
    everlastingness of, O it is an all youth!
Come then, your ways and airs and looks, locks,
    maidengear, gallantry and gaiety and grace,
Winning ways, airs innocent, maiden manners, sweet   15
    looks, loose locks, long locks, lovelocks, gaygear,
    going gallant, girlgrace—
Resign them, sign them, seal them, send them, motion
    them with breath,
And with sighs soaring, soaring síghs deliver
Them; beauty-in-the-ghost, deliver it, early now, long
    before death

Give beauty back, beauty, beauty, beauty, back to God,
    beauty's self and beauty's giver.
See; not a hair is, not an eyelash, not the least lash lost;   20
    every hair
Is, hair of the head, numbered.
Nay, what we had lighthanded left in surly the mere
    mould
Will have waked and have waxed and have walked with
    the wind what while we slept,
This side, that side hurling a heavyheaded hundredfold
What while we, while we slumbered.   25
O then, weary then whý should we tread? O why are we
    so haggard at the heart, so care-coiled, care-killed, so
    fagged, so fashed, so cogged, so cumbered,
When the thing we freely fórfeit is kept with fonder a
    care,
Fonder a care kept than we could have kept it, kept
Far with fonder a care (and we, we should have lost it)
    finer, fonder
A care kept.—Where kept? Do but tell us where kept,   30
    where—
Yonder.—What high as that! We follow, now we follow.—
    Yonder, yes yonder, yonder,
Yonder.

The Blessed Virgin compared
to the Air we Breathe

    Wild air, world-mothering air,
    Nestling me everywhere,
    That each eyelash or hair

Girdles; goes home betwixt
The fleeciest, frailest-flixed   5
Snowflake; that's fairly mixed
With, riddles, and is rife
In every least thing's life;
This needful, never spent,
And nursing element;   10
My more than meat and drink,
My meal at every wink;
This air, which, by life's law,
My lung must draw and draw
Now but to breathe its praise,   15
Minds me in many ways
Of her who not only
Gave God's infinity
Dwindled to infancy
Welcome in womb and breast,   20
Birth, milk, and all the rest
But mothers each new grace
That does now reach our race—
Mary Immaculate,
Merely a woman, yet   25
Whose presence, power is
Great as no goddess's
Was deemèd, dreamèd; who
This one work has to do—
Let all God's glory through,   30
God's glory which would go
Through her and from her flow
    Off, and no way but so.

    I say that we are wound
With mercy round and round   35

As if with air: the same
Is Mary, more by name.
She, wild web, wondrous robe,
Mantles the guilty globe,
Since God has let dispense   40
Her prayers his providence:
Nay, more than almoner,
The sweet alms' self is her
And men are meant to share
Her life as life does air.   45
 If I have understood,
She holds high motherhood
Towards all our ghostly good
And plays in grace her part
About man's beating heart,   50
Laying, like air's fine flood,
The deathdance in his blood;
Yet no part but what will
Be Christ our Saviour still.
Of her flesh he took flesh: 55
He does take fresh and fresh,
Though much the mystery how,
Not flesh but spirit now
And makes, O marvellous!
New Nazareths in us,   60
Where she shall yet conceive
Him, morning, noon, and eve;
New Bethlems, and he born
There, evening, noon, and morn—
Bethlem or Nazareth,   65
Men here may draw like breath
More Christ and baffle death;
Who, born so, comes to be

New self and nobler me
In each one and each one 70
More makes, when all is done,
Both God's and Mary's Son.
    Again, look overhead
How air is azurèd;
O how! Nay do but stand 75
Where you can lift your hand
Skywards: rich, rich it laps
Round the four fingergaps.
Yet such a sapphire-shot,
Charged, steepèd sky will not 80
Stain light. Yea, mark you this:
It does no prejudice.
The glass-blue days are those
When every colour glows,
Each shape and shadow shows. 85
Blue be it: this blue heaven
The seven or seven times seven
Hued sunbeam will transmit
Perfect, not alter it.
Or if there does some soft, 90
On things aloof, aloft,
Bloom breathe, that one breath more
Earth is the fairer for.
Whereas did air not make
This bath of blue and slake 95
His fire, the sun would shake,
A blear and blinding ball
With blackness bound, and all
The thick stars round him roll
Flashing like flecks of coal, 100
Quartz-fret, or sparks of salt,

In grimy vasty vault.
     So God was god of old:
A mother came to mould
Those limbs like ours which are   105
What must make our daystar
Much dearer to mankind;
Whose glory bare would blind
Or less would win man's mind.
Through her we may see him   110
Made sweeter, not made dim,
And her hand leaves his light
Sifted to suit our sight.
     Be thou then, O thou dear
Mother, my atmosphere;   115
My happier world, wherein
To wend and meet no sin;
Above me, round me lie
Fronting my froward eye
With sweet and scarless sky;   120
Stir in my ears, speak there
Of God's love, O live air,
Of patience, penance, prayer:
World-mothering air, air wild,
Wound with thee, in thee isled,   125
Fold home, fast fold thy child.

Spelt from Sibyl's Leaves

Earnest, earthless, equal, attuneable, ¹ vaulty, voluminous, . . .
     stupendous
Evening strains to be tíme's vást, ¹ womb-of-all, home-of-all,
     hearse-of-all night.

Her fond yellow hornlight wound to the west, ' her wild
  hollow hoarlight hung to the height
Waste; her earliest stars, earlstars, ' stárs principal,
  overbend us,
Fíre-féaturing heaven. For earth ' her being has unbound; 5
  her dapple is at an end, as—
tray or aswarm, all throughther, in throngs; ' self ín self
  steepèd and páshed—qúite
Disremembering, dísmémbering ' áll now. Heart, you
  round me right
With: Óur évening is over us; óur night ' whélms, whélms,
  ánd will end us.
Only the beakleaved boughs dragonish ' damask the
  tool-smooth bleak light; black,
Ever so black on it. Óur tale, O óur oracle! ' Lét life, 10
  wáned, ah lét life wind
Off hér once skéined stained véined varíety ' upon, áll on
  twó spools; párt, pen, páck
Now her áll in twó flocks, twó folds—black, white; '
  right, wrong; reckon but, reck but, mind
But thése two; wáre of a wórld where bút these ' twó tell,
  each off the óther; of a rack
Where, selfwrung, selfstrung, sheathe- and shelterless, '
  thóughts agaínst thoughts ín groans grínd.

To what serves Mortal Beauty?

To what serves mortal beauty ' —dangerous; does set dancing blood—the O-seal-that-so ' feature, flung prouder form
Than Purcell tune lets tread to? ' See: it does this: keeps
  warm

Men's wits to the things that are; ¹ what good means—
    where a glance
Master more may than gaze, ¹ gaze out of countenance.   5
Those lovely lads once, wet-fresh ¹ windfalls of war's
    storm,
How then should Gregory, a father, ¹ have gleanèd else
    from swarm-
ed Rome? But God to a nation ¹ dealt that day's dear
    chance.
      To man, that needs would worship ¹ block or barren
        stone,
Our law says: Love what are ¹ love's worthiest, were all   10
    known;
World's loveliest—men's selves. Self ¹ flashes off frame and
    face.
What do then? how meet beauty? ¹ Merely meet it; own,
Home at heart, heaven's sweet gift; ¹ then leave, let that
    alone.
Yea, wish that though, wish all, ¹ God's better beauty,
    grace.

The Soldier

Yes. Whý do we áll, seeing of a soldier, bless him? bless
Our redcoats, óur tars? Both these being, the greater part,
But frail clay, nay but foul clay. Here it is: the heart,
Since, proud, it calls the calling manly, gives a guess
That, hopes that, makesbelieve, the men must be no less;   5
It fancies, feigns, deems, dears the artist after his art;
And fain will find as sterling all as all is smart,
And scarlet wear the spirit of wár thére express.

Mark Christ our King. He knows war, served this
   soldiering through;
He of all can reeve a rope best. There he bides in bliss   10
Now, and séeing somewhére some mán do all that man can
   do,
For love he leans forth, needs his neck must fall on, kiss,
And cry 'O Christ-done deed! So God-made-flesh does too:
Were I come o'er again' cries Christ 'it should be this'.

Carrion Comfort

Not, I'll not, carrion comfort, Despair, not feast on thee;
Not untwist—slack they may be—these last strands of man
In me ór, most weary, cry *I can no more*. I can;
Can something, hope, wish day come, not choose not to be.
But ah, but O thou terrible, why wouldst thou rude on me
Thy wring-world right foot rock? lay a lionlimb against   6
   me? scan
With darksome devouring eyes my bruisèd bones? and fan,
O in turns of tempest, me heaped there; me frantic to
   avoid thee and flee?

   Why? That my chaff might fly; my grain lie, sheer and
      clear.
Nay in all that toil, that coil, since (seems) I kissed the rod, 10
Hand rather, my heart lo! lapped strength, stole joy,
   would laugh, chéer.
Cheer whom though? the hero whose heaven-handling
   flung me, fóot tród
Me? or me that fought him? O which one? is it each one? That
   night, that year
Of now done darkness I wretch lay wrestling with (my
   God!) my God.

'No worst, there is none'

No worst, there is none. Pitched past pitch of grief,
More pangs will, schooled at forepangs, wilder wring.
Comforter, where, where is your comforting?
Mary, mother of us, where is your relief?
My cries heave, herds-long; huddle in a main, a chief-   5
woe, wórld-sorrow; on an áge-old anvil wince and sing—
Then lull, then leave off. Fury had shrieked 'No ling-
ering! Let me be fell: force I must be brief'.

   O the mind, mind has mountains; cliffs of fall
Frightful, sheer, no-man-fathomed. Hold them cheap   10
May who ne'er hung there. Nor does long our small
Durance deal with that steep or deep. Here! creep,
Wretch, under a comfort serves in a whirlwind: all
Life death does end and each day dies with sleep.

'To seem the stranger lies my lot'

To seem the stranger lies my lot, my life
Among strangers. Father and mother dear,
Brothers and sisters are in Christ not near
And he my peace/my parting, sword and strife.
   England, whose honour O all my heart woos, wife   5
To my creating thought, would neither hear
Me, were I pleading, plead nor do I: I wear-
y of idle a being but by where wars are rife.
   I am in Ireland now; now I am at a thírd
Remove. Not but in all removes I can   10
Kind love both give and get. Only what word
Wisest my heart breeds dark heaven's baffling ban
Bars or hell's spell thwarts. This to hoard unheard,
Heard unheeded, leaves me a lonely began.

'I wake and feel the fell of dark'

I wake and feel the fell of dark, not day.
What hours, O what black hoürs we have spent
This night! what sights you, heart, saw; ways you went!
And more must, in yet longer light's delay.
   With witness I speak this. But where I say   5
Hours I mean years, mean life. And my lament
Is cries countless, cries like dead letters sent
To dearest him that lives alas! away.

I am gall, I am heartburn. God's most deep decree
Bitter would have me taste: my taste was me;   10
Bones built in me, flesh filled, blood brimmed the curse.
   Selfyeast of spirit a dull dough sours. I see
The lost are like this, and their scourge to be
As I am mine, their sweating selves; but worse.

'Patience, hard thing!'

Patience, hard thing! the hard thing but to pray,
But bid for, Patience is! Patience who asks
Wants war, wants wounds; weary his times, his tasks;
To do without, take tosses, and obey.
   Rare patience roots in these, and, these away,   5
Nowhere. Natural heart's ivy, Patience masks
Our ruins of wrecked past purpose. There she basks
Purple eyes and seas of liquid leaves all day.

We hear our hearts grate on themselves: it kills
To bruise them dearer. Yet the rebellious wills   10
Of us we do bid God bend to him even so.
   And where is he who more and more distils
Delicious kindness?—He is patient. Patience fills
His crisp combs, and that comes those ways we know.

'My own heart let me more have pity on'

My own heart let me more have pity on; let
Me live to my sad self hereafter kind,
Charitable; not live this tormented mind
With this tormented mind tormenting yet.
   I cast for comfort I can no more get   5
By groping round my comfortless, than blind
Eyes in their dark can day or thirst can find
Thirst's all-in-all in all a world of wet.

Soul, self; come, poor Jackself, I do advise
You, jaded, let be; call off thoughts awhile   10
Elsewhere; leave comfort root-room; let joy size
At God knows when to God knows what; whose smile
's not wrung, see you; unforeseen times rather—as skies
Betweenpie mountains—lights a lovely mile.

Tom's Garland:

upon the Unemployed

Tom—garlanded with squat and surly steel
Tom; then Tom's fallowbootfellow piles pick
By him and rips out rockfire homeforth—sturdy Dick;
Tom Heart-at-ease, Tom Navvy: he is all for his meal

Sure, 's bed now. Low be it: lustily he his low lot (feel   5
That ne'er need hunger, Tom; Tom seldom sick,
Seldomer heartsore; that treads through, prickproof, thick
Thousands of thorns, thoughts) swings though. Commonweal
Little í reck ho! lacklevel in, if all had bread:
What! Country is honour enough in all us—lordly head,   10
With heaven's lights high hung round, or, mother-ground
That mammocks, mighty foot. But nó way sped,
Nor mind nor mainstrength; gold go garlanded
With, perilous, O nó; nor yet plod safe shod sound;
                    Undenizened, beyond bound   15
Of earth's glory, earth's ease, all; no one, nowhere,
In wide the world's weal; rare gold, bold steel, bare
                    In both; care, but share care—
This, by Despair, bred Hangdog dull; by Rage,
Manwolf, worse; and their packs infest the age.   20

Harry Ploughman

Hard as hurdle arms, with a broth of goldish flue,
Breathed round; the rack of ribs; the scooped flank; lank
Rope-over thigh; knee-nave; and barrelled shank—
                    Head and foot, shoulder and shank—
By a grey eye's head steered well, one crew, fall to;   5
Stand at stress. Each limb's barrowy brawn, his thew
That onewhere curded, onewhere sucked or sank—
                    Soared or sank—,
Though as a beechbole firm, finds his, as at a roll-call, rank
And features, in flesh, what deed he each must do—   10
                    His sinew-service where do.

He leans to it, Harry bends, look. Back, elbow, and liquid
    waist
In him, all quail to the wallowing o' the plough: 's cheek
    crimsons; curls
Wag or crossbridle, in a wind lifted, windlaced—
                 See his wind- lilylocks -laced;   15
Churlsgrace, too, child of Amansstrength, how it hangs or
    hurls
Them—broad in bluff hide his frowning feet lashed! raced
With, along them, cragiron under and cold furls—
              With-a-fountain's shining-shot furls.

That Nature is a Heraclitean Fire
and of the
comfort of the Resurrection

Cloud-puffball, torn tufts, tossed pillows ' flaunt forth,
    then chevy on an air-
built thoroughfare: heaven-roysterers, in gay-gangs ' they
    throng; they glitter in marches.
Down roughcast, down dazzling whitewash, ' wherever
    an elm arches,
Shivelights and shadowtackle in long ' lashes lace, lance, and
    pair.
Delightfully the bright wind boisterous ' ropes, wrestles,   5
    beats earth bare
Of yestertempest's creases; ' in pool and rutpeel parches
Squandering ooze to squeezed ' dough, crust, dust; stanches,
    starches
Squadroned masks and manmarks ' treadmire toil there

Footfretted in it. Million-fuelèd, ⎪ nature's bonfire burns on.
But quench her bonniest, dearest ⎪ to her, her clearest-   10
  selvèd spark
Man, how fast his firedint, ⎪ his mark on mind, is gone!
Both are in an unfathomable, all is in an enormous dark
Drowned. O pity and indig ⎪ nation! Manshape, that shone
Sheer off, disseveral, a star, ⎪ death blots black out; nor mark
        Is any of him at all so stark   15
But vastness blurs and time ⎪beats level. Enough! the
  Resurrection,
A heart's-clarion! Away grief's gasping, ⎪ joyless days,
  dejection.
        Across my foundering deck shone
A beacon, an eternal beam. ⎪ Flesh fade, and mortal trash
Fall to the residuary worm; ⎪ world's wildfire, leave   20
  but ash:
        In a flash, at a trumpet crash,
I am all at once what Christ is, ⎪ since he was what I am, and
This Jack, joke, poor potsherd, ⎪ patch, matchwood,
  immortal diamond,
        Is immortal diamond.

In honour of

St. Alphonsus Rodriguez

Laybrother of the Society of Jesus

Honour is flashed off exploit, so we say;
And those strokes once that gashed flesh or galled shield
Should tongue that time now, trumpet now that field,
And, on the fighter, forge his glorious day.
On Christ they do and on the martyr may;   5
But be the war within, the brand we wield
Unseen, the heroic breast not outward-steeled,
Earth hears no hurtle then from fiercest fray.

Yet God (that hews mountain and continent,
Earth, all, out; who, with trickling increment,   10
Veins violets and tall trees makes more and more)
Could crowd career with conquest while there went
Those years and years by of world without event
That in Majorca Alfonso watched the door.

'Thou art indeed just, Lord'

*Justus quidem tu es, Domine, si disputem tecum; verumtamen justa
loquar ad te: Quare via impiorum prosperatur? &c.*

Thou art indeed just, Lord, if I contend
With thee; but, sir, so what I plead is just.
Why do sinners' ways prosper? and why must
Disappointment all I endeavour end?

Wert thou my enemy, O thou my friend,   5
How wouldst thou worse, I wonder, than thou dost
Defeat, thwart me? Oh, the sots and thralls of lust
Do in spare hours more thrive than I that spend,
Sir, life upon thy cause. See, banks and brakes
Now, leavèd how thick! lacèd they are again   10
With fretty chervil, look, and fresh wind shakes
Them; birds build—but not I build; no, but strain,
Time's eunuch, and not breed one work that wakes.
Mine, O thou lord of life, send my roots rain.

'The shepherd's brow'

The shepherd's brow, fronting forked lightning, owns
The horror and the havoc and the glory
Of it. Angels fall, they are towers, from heaven—a story
Of just, majestical, and giant groans.
But man—we, scaffold of score brittle bones;   5
Who breathe, from groundlong babyhood to hoary
Age gasp; whose breath is our *memento mori*—
What bass is *our* viol for tragic tones?
He! Hand to mouth he lives, and voids with shame;
And, blazoned in however bold the name,   10
Man Jack the man is, just; his mate a hussy.
And I that die these deaths, that feed this flame,
That . . . in smooth spoons spy life's masque mirrored: tame
My tempests there, my fire and fever fussy.

To R. B.

The fine delight that fathers thought; the strong
Spur, live and lancing like the blowpipe flame,
Breathes once and, quenchèd faster than it came,
Leaves yet the mind a mother of immortal song.
Nine months she then, nay years, nine years she long
Within her wears, bears, cares and combs the same:
The widow of an insight lost she lives, with aim
Now known and hand at work now never wrong.
  Sweet fire the sire of muse, my soul needs this;
I want the one rapture of an inspiration.   10
O then if in my lagging lines you miss
The roll, the rise, the carol, the creation,
My winter world, that scarcely breathes that bliss
Now, yields you, with some sighs, our explanation.

SELECTIONS FROM UNFINISHED POEMS AND FRAGMENTS
(1876-89)

The Woodlark

Teevo cheevo cheevio chee:
O where, what can thát be?
Weedio-weedio: there again!
So tiny a trickle of sóng-strain;

And all round not to be found   5
For brier, bough, furrow, or gréen ground
Before or behind or far or at hand
Either left either right
Anywhere in the súnlight.

Well, after all! Ah but hark—   10
'I am the little wóodlark.
The skylark is my cousin and he
Is known to men more than me.
Round a ring, around a ring
And while I sail (must listen) I sing.   15

To-day the sky is two and two
With white strokes and strains of the blue.
The blue wheat-acre is underneath
And the corn is corded and shoulders its sheaf,
The ear in milk, lush the sash,   20
And crush-silk poppies aflash,
The blood-gush blade-gash
Flame-rash rudred
Bud shelling or broad-shed
Tatter-tangled and dingle-a-danglèd   25
Dandy-hung dainty head.

And down . . . the furrow dry
Sunspurge and oxeye
And lace-leaved lovely
Foam-tuft fumitory.   30

I ám so véry, O só very glád
That I dó thínk there is not to be had
[Anywhere any more joy to be in.
Cheevio:] when the cry within

Hнs

Says Go on then I go on 35
Till the longing is less and the good gone,
But down drop, if it says Stop,
To the all-a-leaf of the tréetop.
And after that off the bough
[Hover-float to the hedge brow.] 40

Through the velvety wind V-winged
[Where shake shadow is sun's-eye-ringed]
To the nest's nook I balance and buoy
With a sweet joy of a sweet joy,
Sweet, of a sweet, of a sweet joy 45
Of a sweet—a sweet—sweet—joy.'

On the Portrait of Two Beautiful Young People

A Brother and Sister

O I admire and sorrow! The heart's eye grieves
Discovering you, dark tramplers, tyrant years.
A juice rides rich through bluebells, in vine leaves,
And beauty's dearest veriest vein is tears.

Happy the father, mother of these! Too fast: 5
Not that, but thus far, all with frailty, blest
In one fair fall; but, for time's aftercast,
Creatures all heft, hope, hazard, interest.

And are they thus? The fine, the fingering beams
Their young delightful hour do feature down 10
That fleeted else like day-dissolvèd dreams
Or ringlet-race on burling Barrow brown.

She leans on him with such contentment fond
As well the sister sits, would well the wife;
His looks, the soul's own letters, see beyond,   15
Gaze on, and fall directly forth on life.

But ah, bright forelock, cluster that you are
Of favoured make and mind and health and youth,
Where lies your landmark, seamark, or soul's star?
There's none but truth can stead you. Christ is truth.   20

There's none but good can bé good, both for you
And what sways with you, maybe this sweet maid;
None good but God—a warning wavèd to
One once that was found wanting when Good weighed.

Man lives that list, that leaning in the will   25
No wisdom can forecast by gauge or guess,
The selfless self of self, most strange, most still,
Fast furled and all foredrawn to No or Yes.

Your feast of; that most in you earnest eye
May but call on your banes to more carouse.   30
Worst will the best. What worm was here, we cry,
To have havoc-pocked so, see, the hung-heavenward
   boughs?

Enough: corruption was the world's first woe.
What need I strain my heart beyond my ken?
O but I bear my burning witness though   35
Against the wild and wanton work of men.

    .   .   .   .

Epithalamion

Hark, hearer, hear what I do; lend a thought now, make
   believe
We are leafwhelmed somewhere with the hood
Of some branchy bunchy bushybowered wood,
Southern dean or Lancashire clough or Devon cleave,
That leans along the loins of hills, where a candycoloured,   5
   where a gluegold-brown
Marbled river, boisterously beautiful, between
Roots and rocks is danced and dandled, all in froth and
   water-blowballs, down.
We are there, when we hear a shout
That the hanging honeysuck, the dogeared hazels in the
   cover
Makes dither, makes hover   10
And the riot of a rout
Of, it must be, boys from the town
Bathing: it is summer's sovereign good.

By there comes a listless stranger: beckoned by the noise
He drops towards the river: unseen   15
Sees the bevy of them, how the boys
With dare and with downdolphinry and bellbright bodies
   huddling out,
Are earthworld, airworld, waterworld thorough hurled,
   all by turn and turn about.

This garland of their gambol flashes in his breast
Into such a sudden zest   20
Of summertime joys

That he hies to a pool neighbouring; sees it is the best
There; sweetest, freshest, shadowiest;
Fairyland; silk-beech, scrolled ash, packed sycamore, wild
   wychelm, hornbeam fretty overstood
By. Rafts and rafts of flake leaves light, dealt so, painted   25
   on the air,
Hang as still as hawk or hawkmoth, as the stars or as the
   angels there,
Like the thing that never knew the earth, never off roots
Rose. Here he feasts: lovely all is! No more: off with—
   down he dings
His bleachèd both and woolwoven wear:
Careless these in coloured wisp   30
All lie tumbled-to; then with loop-locks
Forward falling, forehead frowning, lips crisp
Over finger-teasing task, his twiny boots
Fast he opens, last he off wrings
Till walk the world he can with bare his feet   35
And come where lies a coffer, burly all of blocks
Built of chancequarrièd, selfquainèd, hoar-huskèd rocks
And the water warbles over into, filleted with glassy
   grassy quicksilvery shivès and shoots
And with heavenfallen freshness down from moorland
   still brims,
Dark or daylight on and on. Here he will then, here he   40
   will the fleet
Flinty kindcold element let break across his limbs
Long. Where we leave him, froliclavish, while he looks
   about him, laughs, swims.

Enough now; since the sacred matter that I mean
I should be wronging longer leaving it to float
Upon this only gambolling and echoing-of-earth note—   45

What is . . . the delightful dean?
Wedlock. What the water? Spousal love.

.   .   .   .

.   .   .   .   turns
Father, mother, brothers, sisters, friends
Into fairy trees, wildflowers, woodferns
Rankèd round the bower   50

.   .   .   .

PROSE

EXTRACTS FROM OXFORD DIARIES
(1864-6)

[*1864*]

Hawk, is sell about the streets. I had imagined this to be
derived from the bawling or screeching the hawkers made in
proclaiming their wares, to *hawk* meaning to make a noise in
the throat, as before spitting. But Kingsley uses a word to
hawk of birds in sense of to move up and down in a place, to   5
haunt. The above sense may be derived from this. He also uses
a verb to *howk* in sense of to harry and with this perhaps is
connected the bird *hawk*.

Lasher from a canal at Wolvercote. The water running
down the lasher violently swells in a massy wave against the   10
opposite bank, which, to resist its force, is defended by a piece
of brick wall. The shape of wave of course bossy, smooth
and globy. Full of bubble and air, very liquid.—For the rest
of the lasher, all except the shoulder where it first sweeps
over it is covered with a kind of silver links. Running like   15
a wind or element at the shoulder.

Note on green wheat. The difference between this green
and that of long grass is that first suggests silver, latter azure.
Former more opacity, body, smoothness. It is the exact
complement of carnation. Nearest to emerald of any green   20

I know, the real emerald *stone*. It is lucent. Perhaps it has a chrysoprase bloom. Both blue greens.

Poetry at Oxford.

It is a happy thing that there is no royal road to poetry. The world should know by this time that one cannot reach Parnassus except by flying thither. Yet from time to time more men go up and either perish in its gullies fluttering *excelsior* flags or else come down again with full folios and blank countenances. Yet the old fallacy keeps its ground. Every age has its false alarms.

Sept. 14. Grey clouds in knops. A curious fan of this kind of cloud radiating from a crown, and covering half the sky.

Sk and *sc* are notoriously often exchanged for *sh*, as *bushy, bosky; rush, ruscus.* So δίσκος may be same word as *dish*, particularly as the ancient quoit was not a flat ring but a plate, a disc.

The sky minted into golden sequins.
Stars like gold tufts.
— — golden bees.
— — golden rowels.
Sky peak'd with tiny flames.
Stars like tiny-spoked wheels of fire.
Lantern of night, pierced in eyelets, (*or* eye-lets which avoids ambiguity.)
Altogether *peak* is a good word. For sunlight through shutter, locks of hair, rays in brass knobs etc. Meadows peaked with flowers.

   His gilded rowels
  Now stars of blood.

 Tuncks is a good name.   50
 Gerard Manley Tuncks. Pook Tuncks.

 Spring from the branch-heads ordering the bright rows
—the leaves, chiefly of the elm

  A star most spiritual, principal, preeminent
  Of all the golden press.   55

    February–March 1865
 Whorlèd wave, whelkèd wave,—and drift.

 Crocus-candles yellow and white.
 Notes for poetry. Feathery rows of young corn. Ruddy,
furred and branchy tops of the elms backed by rolling cloud. 60
 Frieze of sculpture, long-membered vines tugged at by
reaching pursuant fauns, and lilies.

 March 12. A day of the great mercy of God.

 Viol-headed, lute-headed, trees.

 Mems. The opposite sunset. The barrow clouds. The 65
valves. The rail. Mallowy. Peace. Valvèd eyes. Bats' wings
and images. Lobes of leaf. Theory of trees. Temper in art.

 He shook with racing notes the standing air.

 Ash clusters like grapes.
 Water rushing over a sunken stone and hollowing itself 70

to rise again seems to be devoured by the wave before which
it forces up,
>   Reverted, with thrown-back and tossing cape.
Bossy water, bosses.
Oak roots are silvery, smooth, solid and muscular.   75
>   Glazed water vaulted o'er a drowsy stone.

Nov. 6. On this day by God's grace I resolved to give up all
beauty until I had His leave for it;—also Dolben's letter came
for which Glory to God.

>   The stars were packed so close that night   80
>   They seemed to press and stare
>   And gather in like hurdles bright
>   The liberties of air.

January 23, 1866

For Lent. No pudding on Sundays. No tea except if to   85
keep me awake and then without sugar. Meat only once a day.
No verses in Passion Week or on Fridays. No lunch or
meat on Fridays. Not to sit in armchair except can work
in no other way. Ash Wednesday and Good Friday bread
and water.   90

Drops of rain hanging on rails etc seen with only the lower
rim lighted like nails (of fingers). Screws of brooks and
twines. Soft chalky look with more shadowy middles of the
globes of cloud on a night with a moon faint or concealed.
Mealy clouds with a not brilliant moon. Blunt buds of the   95
ash. Pencil buds of the beech. Lobes of the trees. Cups of
the eyes. Gathering back the lightly hinged eyelids. Bows
of the eyelids. Pencil of eyelashes. Juices of the eyeball. Eyelids
like leaves, petals, caps, tufted hats, handkerchiefs, sleeves,

gloves. Also of the bones sleeved in flesh. Juices of the sunrise. 100
Join and veins of the same. Vermilion look of the hand held
against a candle with the darker parts as the middles of the
fingers and especially the knuckles covered with ash.

————————

EXTRACTS FROM THE JOURNAL
(1866-75)

May 3 [1866].... Walked then with Addis, crossing Bablock
Hythe, round by Skinner's Weir through many fields into the
Witney Road. Sky sleepy blue without liquidity. From
Cumnor Hill saw St. Philip's and the other spires through
blue haze rising pale in a pink light. On further side of the   5
Witney road hills, just fleeced with grain or other green
growth, by their dips and waves foreshortened here and
there and so differenced in brightness and opacity the green
on them, with delicate effect. On left, brow of the near hill
glistening with very bright newly turned sods and a scarf   10
of vivid green slanting away beyond the skyline, against which
the clouds shewed the slightest tinge of rose or purple.
Copses in grey-red or grey-yellow—the tinges immediately
forerunning the opening of full leaf. Meadows skirting
Seven-bridge road voluptuous green. Some oaks are out   15
in small leaf. Ashes not out, only tufted with their fringy
blooms. Hedges springing richly. Elms in small leaf, with
more or less opacity. White poplars most beautiful in small
grey crisp spray-like leaf. Cowslips capriciously colouring
meadows in creamy drifts. Bluebells, purple orchis. Over the   20
green water of the river passing the slums of the town and
under its bridges swallows shooting, blue and purple above

and shewing their amber-tinged breasts reflected in the water, their flight unsteady with wagging wings and leaning first to one side and then the other. Peewits flying. Towards sunset the sky partly swept, as often, with moist white cloud, tailing off across which are morsels of grey-black woolly clouds. Sun seemed to make a bright liquid hole in this, its texture had an upward northerly sweep or drift from the W. marked softly in grey. Dog violets. Eastward after sunset range of clouds rising in bulky heads moulded softly in tufts or bunches of snow—so it looks—and membered somewhat elaborately, rose-coloured. Notice often imperfect fairy rings. Apple and other fruit trees blossomed beautifully. A. talking about the whole story of the home affairs. His idea was (when he went down three years ago and was all the Long preparing for confession) that 7 years was a moderate time during which to fast within the boundaries of life and abstain from communicating. Being not allowed to read he took long walks, and it must have been on one of these that he fainted as he once told me. . . .

May 6. Grey. A little time ago on much such another day noticed Trinity gardens. Much distinctness, charm, and suggestiveness about the match of white grey sky, solid smooth lawn, firs and yews, dark trees, below, and chestnuts and other brighter-hued trees above, the young green having a fresh, moist opaque look and there being in the whole picture an absence of projection, and apprehension of colour. On such a day also last Friday week boated with H. Dugmore to Godstow, but the warm greyness of the day, the river, the spring green, and the cuckoo wanted a canon by which to harmonize and round them in—e.g. one of feeling.

May 15. . . . Walking in Magdalen walks. Green-white of lower leafage especially in elms and beeches: of course in the beeches it is almost the natural hue. Elm trunks are blue or

purple rich moist black at this time, as thrown out by the
thick heaps and armfuls of the wet pellets of young green of
which their leafing now 'stands'. To see the long forward-
creeping curls of the newly-leaved trees, in sweeps and
rows all lodged one with another down the meadow edge, 60
beautiful, but distraction and the want of the canon only
makes these graceful shapes in the keen unseasonable evening
air to 'carve out' one's thought with painful definiteness.
Hemlock in clouds of bloom. The shallow shelves of beech
branches hang with light and certain poise, dividing the air, 65
say just over one's head, with level-grown pieces of pale
window-like green spotted with soft darks by the now and
then overlapping of the leaves. . . .

June 3. . . . Clouds growing in beauty at end of the day. In
the afternoon a white rack of two parallel spines, vertebrated 70
as so often. At sunset, when the sky had charm and beauty,
very level clouds, long pelletted sticks of shade-softened grey
in the West, with gold-colour splashed sunset-spot, then
more to the S. grey rows rather thicker and their oblique flake
or thread better marked, above them on a ground of indis- 75
tincter grey a drift of spotty tufts or drops, a 'dirty' looking
kind of clouds, scud-like, rising.

June 13. Commemoration. . . . Was happily able to see
composition of the crowd in the area of the theatre, all the
heads looking one way thrown up by their black coats 80
relieved only by white shirt-fronts etc; the short strokes
of eyes, nose, mouth, repeated hundreds of times I believe
it is which gives the visible law: looked at in any one instance
it flies. I could find a sort of beauty in this, certainly character
—but in fact that is almost synonymous with finding order, 85
anywhere. The short parallel strokes spoken of are like those
something in effect on the cusp-ends of six-foils in the iron
tracery of the choir gates in our chapel.

July 11. . . . . Oats: hoary blue-green sheaths and stalks, prettily shadow-stroked spikes of pale green grain. Oaks: the 90 organization of this tree is difficult. Speaking generally no doubt the determining planes are concentric, a system of brief contiguous and continuous tangents, whereas those of the cedar would roughly be called horizontals and those of the beech radiating but modified by droop and by a screw-set 95 towards jutting points. But beyond this since the normal growth of the boughs is radiating and the leaves grow some way in there is of course a system of spoke-wise clubs of green—sleeve-pieces. And since the end shoots curl and carry young and scanty leaf-stars these clubs are tapered, and I have 100 seen also the pieces in profile with chiselled outlines, the blocks thus made detached and lessening towards the end. However the star knot is the chief thing: it is whorled, worked round, a little and this is what keeps up the illusion of the tree: the leaves are rounded inwards and figure out ball-knots. Oaks 105 differ much, and much turns on the broadness of the leaf, the narrower giving the crisped and starry and catharine-wheel forms, the broader the flat-pieced mailed or shard-covered ones, in which it is possible to see composition in dips, etc., on wider bases than the single knot or cluster. But I shall study 110 them further. See the 19th.

July 19. . . . . Alone in the woods and in Mr. Nelthorpe's park, whence one gets such a beautiful view southwards over the country. I have now found the law of the oak leaves. It is of platter-shaped stars altogether; the leaves lie close like 115 pages, packed, and as if drawn tightly to. But these old packs, which lie at the end of their twigs, throw out now long shoots alternately and slimly leaved, looking like bright keys. All the sprays but markedly these ones shape out and as it were embrace greater circles and the dip and toss of these makes the 120 wider and less organic articulations of the tree.

Aug. 22 [*1867*]. For July 6, 1866 I have a note on elm-leaves, that they sit crisp, dark, glossy, and saddle-shaped along their twigs, on which at that time an inner frill of soft juicy young leaves had just been run; they chip the sky, and where their waved edge turns downwards they gleam and blaze like an underlip sometimes will when seen against the light.

Aug. 30. . . . A round by Plumley.—Stands of ash in a copse: they consisted of two or three rods most gracefully leaved, for each wing or comb finally curled inwards, that is upwards.—Putting my hand up against the sky whilst we lay on the grass I saw more richness and beauty in the blue than I had known of before, not brilliance but glow and colour. It was not transparent and sapphire-like, but turquoise-like, swarming and blushing round the edge of the hand and in the pieces clipped in by the fingers, the flesh being sometimes sunlit, sometimes glassy with reflected light, sometimes lightly shadowed in that violet one makes with cobalt and Indian red.

Apr. [*1868*]. . . . A budded lime against the field wall: turn, pose, and counter-point in the twigs and buds—the *form* speaking.

June 16. . . . Honeysuckle at the hedge on the big bank in bloom, the crests coiled back into a crown, the tongues or spurs curled at heel, the lashes (anthers) giving off all round: this is their time of greatest beauty. They look gold or honey colour.—Gold too is the colour of the fringes in the middle of the syringa.—The passage of the roses through the following scale of colours, perhaps from the dryness of the season, most marked—scarlet, blood-colour, crimson, purple, then the red retiring to the shaded or inner part of the petal the outer or coiled part bleaches lilac or greenish.

June 27. Silver mottled clouding, and clearer: else like yesterday. At the National Gallery. That Madonna by

Beltraffio. Query has not Giotto the instress of loveliness? 155
Mantegna's draperies.

July 3. . . . Started with Ed. Bond for Switzerland. We went
by Dover and Ostende to Brussels.

July 7. . . . Swiss trees are, like English, well inscaped—in
quains. 160

July 8. . . . From Lucerne by steamer to Kussnacht, thence
walk across to Immensee, thence by steamer over lake of
Zug to Arth, whence up the Rigi.—The normal colour of the
lake water, from near at least, bottle blue; from some way up
we saw it with the sea shoaling colours, purple and blue, 165
the purple expressing the rose of the chord to the eye (—in
the same way as the same colour in a rose fading expresses
the blue of the chord—the converse case: in fact it may
perhaps be generalized that when this happens the modulation
in question is the flat of the next term and not the sharp of the 170
former one). From the top the lakes egg-blue, blue strongly
modulated to green.—At sunset featherbed sky with a fluffy
and jointed rib-cloud: I noted one 'flock' of which I made a
drawing was a long time with little change.—Huddling and
precipitation of the fir woods down one side of the Rossberg 175
following the fall of water like the sheepflock at Shanklin did.

July 9. Before sunrise looking out of window saw a noble
scape of stars—the Plough all golden falling, Cassiopeïa
on end with her bright quains pointing to the right, the
graceful bends of Perseus underneath her, and some great star 180
whether Capella or not I am not sure risen over the brow of
the mountain. Sunrise we saw well: the north landscape was
blighty but the south, the important one, with the Alps,
clear; lower down all was mist and flue of white cloud, which
grew thicker as the day went on and like a junket, lay scattered 185
on the lakes. The sun lit up the bright acres of the snows at
first with pink but afterwards clear white: the snow of the

Bernese Highland remained from its distance pinkish all day.
—The mountain ranges, as any series or body of inanimate
like things not often seen, have the air of persons and of 190
interrupted activity; they are multitudinous too, and also
they express a second level with an upper world or shires of
snow.—In going down between Pilatus and a long streak of
cloud the blue was greenish. Since I have found this colour
is seen in looking from the snow to the sky but why I do not 195
understand: can there possibly be a rose hue suppressed in
the white (—*purpurea candidior nive*)?

Alpine cows dun-coloured and very well made. Melodious
lines of a cow's dewlap. . . .

July 13. The Giessbach falls like heaps of snow or like lades 200
of shining rice. The smaller falls in it shew gaily sprigged,
fretted, and curled edges dancing down, like the crispiest
endive.

July 15. . . . There are round one of the heights of the
Jungfrau two ends or falls of a glacier. If you took the skin 205
of a white tiger or the deep fell of some other animal and
swung it tossing high in the air and then cast it out before
you it would fall and so clasp and lap round anything in its
way just as this glacier does and the fleece would part in the
same rifts: you must suppose a lazuli under-flix to appear. The 210
spraying out of one end I tried to catch but it would have
taken hours: it was this which first made me think of a
tiger-skin, and it ends in tongues and points like the tail and
claws: indeed the ends of the glaciers are knotted or knuckled
like talons. Above, in a plane nearly parallel to the eye, 215
becoming thus foreshortened, it forms saddle-curves with
dips and swells. . . .

At Grindelwald are two glaciers, the upper and lower,
which are in fact two descending limbs of one. I shall speak
of them from my knowledge since. Above where the 220

IHS

mountains make hollows they lie saddle-wise in them and then
shouldering through the gorges are broken up—but the
question is whether by the pressure or the slope. In slanted
brooks the bias keeps falling from bank to bank across and
so knits the stream and glaciers also are cross-hatched with 225
their crevasses but they form waves which lie regularly and
in horizontals across the current. (So water does in fact,
wimpling, but these wimplings have the air of being only
resultants or accumulations; perhaps they too are a real
inscape here seen descending and vanishing.) In the gut these 230
glaciers are hollowed in the middle, not rounded up. Below
this they open out and part lengthwise. These Grindelwald
glaciers are remarkable for their ruggedness, I believe: the
upper one looks like rows of dogteeth. The blue colour
(which compared by a glance with the sky is greener) retiring 235
into these clefts looks like starch in ruffs. Becoming deep
within it looks like deep flesh-cuts where one sees the blood
flush and welling up.—We went into the absurd grotto.

July 19. . . . I was arguing about the planing of rocks and
made a sketch of two in the Aar, and after that it was strange, 240
for Nature became Nemesis, so precise they were, and E. B.
himself pointed out two which looked, he said, as if they had
been sawn. And of the hills themselves it could sometimes be
be seen, but on the other hand the sides of the valley often
descended in trending sweeps of vertical section and so met 245
at the bottom.

At times the valley opened in *cirques*, amphitheatres,
enclosing levels of plain, and the river then ran between flaky
flat-fish isles made of cindery lily-white stones.—In or near
one of these openings the guide cries out 'Voulez-vous une 250
Alp-rose?' and up he springs the side of the hill and brings us
each bunches of flowers down.

In one place over a smooth table of rock came slipping

down a blade of water looking like and as evenly crisped
as fruitnets let drop and falling slack.   255

We saw Handeck waterfall. It is in fact the meeting of
two waters, the right the Aar sallow and jade-coloured, the
left a smaller stream of clear lilac foam. It is the greatest fall
we have seen. The lower half is hidden in spray. I watched the
great bushes of foam-water, the texture of branchings and   260
water-spandrils which makes them up. At their outsides
nearest the rock they gave off showers of drops strung together
into little quills which sprang out in fans.

On crossing the Aar again there was as good a fall as some
we have paid to see, all in jostling foam-bags.   265

Across the valley too we saw the fall of the Gelmer—
like milk chasing round blocks of coal; or a girdle or long
purse of white weighted with irregular black rubies, carelessly
thrown aside and lying in jutty bends, with a black clasp of the
same stone at the top—for those were the biggest blocks,   270
squared, and built up, as it happened, in lessening stories,
and the cascade enclosed them on the right and left hand with
its foam; or once more like the skin of a white snake square-
pied with black.

July 20. Fine.   275

Walked down to the Rhone glacier. It has three stages—
first a smoothly-moulded bed in a pan or theatre of thorny
peaks, swells of ice rising through the snow-sheet and the
snow itself tossing and fretting into the sides of the rock walls
in spray-like points: this is the first stage of the glaciers   280
generally; it is like bright-plucked water swaying in a pail—;
second, after a slope nearly covered with landslips of moraine,
was a ruck of horned waves steep and narrow in the gut:
now in the upper Grindelwald glacier between the bed or
highest stage was a descending limb which was like the rude   285
and knotty bossings of a strombus shell—; third the foot, a

broad limb opening out and reaching the plain, shaped like the fan-fin of a dolphin or a great bivalve shell turned on its face, the flutings in either case being suggested by the crevasses and the ribs by the risings between them, these being swerved and inscaped strictly to the motion of the mass. Or you may compare the three stages to the heel, instep, and ball or toes of a foot.—The second stage looked at from nearer appeared like a box of plaster of Paris or starch or tooth-powder, a little moist, tilted up and then struck and jarred so that the powder broke and tumbled in shapes and rifts.

We went into the grotto and also the vault from which the Rhone flows. It looked like a blue tent and as you went further in changed to lilac. As you come out the daylight glazes the groins with gleaming rosecolour. The ice inside has a branchy wire texture. The man shewed us the odd way in which a little piece of ice will stick against the walls—as if drawn by a magnet.

Standing on the glacier saw the prismatic colours in the clouds, and worth saying what sort of clouds; it was fine shapeless skins of fretted make, full of eyebrows or like linings of curled leaves which one finds in shelved corners of a wood.

July 25. . . . Up at two to ascend the Breithorn. Stars twiring brilliantly. Taurus up, a pale light stressily edging the eastern skyline, and lightning mingled with the dawn. In the twilight we tumbled over the moraine and glacier until the sunrise brightly fleshed the snow of the Breithorn before us and then the colour changing through metallic shades of yellow recovered to white.

We were accompanied by a young Mr. Pease of Darlington, his guide Gasser, and ours, Welchen.

From the summit the view on the Italian side was broken by endless ranges of part-vertical dancing cloud, the highest and furthest flaked or foiled like fungus and coloured pink.

But, as the Interlaken Frenchman said, the mountain summits 320
are not the places for mountain views, the things do not look
high when you are as high as they are; beside Monte Rosa,
the Lyskamm, etc. did not make themselves; shape as well
as size went: then the cold feet, the spectacles, the talk, and
the lunching came in. Even with one companion ecstasy is 325
almost banished: you want to be alone and to feel that, and
leisure—all pressure taken off.

Feb.—, 1870. One day in the Long Retreat (which ended
on Xmas Day) they were reading in the refectory Sister
Emmerich's account of the Agony in the Garden and I 330
suddenly began to cry and sob and could not stop. I put it
down for this reason, that if I had been asked a minute
beforehand I should have said that nothing of the sort was
going to happen and even when it did I stood in a manner
wondering at myself not seeing in my reason the traces of an 335
adequate cause for such strong emotion—the traces of it I
say because of course the cause in itself is adequate for the
sorrow of a lifetime. I remember much the same thing on
Maundy Thursday when the presanctified Host was carried
to the sacristy. But neither the weight nor the stress of 340
sorrow, that is to say of the thing which should cause sorrow,
by themselves move us or bring the tears as a sharp knife does
not cut for being pressed as long as it is pressed without any
shaking of the hand but there is always one touch, something
striking sideways and unlooked for, which in both cases 345
undoes resistance and pierces, and this may be so delicate that
the pathos seems to have gone directly to the body and
cleared the understanding in its passage. On the other hand
the pathetic touch by itself, as in dramatic pathos, will only
draw slight tears if its matter is not important or not of 350
import to us, the strong emotion coming from a force which
was gathered before it was discharged: in this way a knife

may pierce the flesh which it had happened only to graze and only grazing will go no deeper.

The winter was called severe. . . . On [Feb.] 9th there was 355 snow but not lying on the roads. On the grass it became a crust lifted on the heads of the blades. As we went down a field near Caesar's Camp I noticed it before me *squalentem*, coat below coat, sketched in intersecting edges bearing 'idiom', all down the slope:—I have no other word yet for that which 360 takes the eye or mind in a bold hand or effective sketching or in marked features or again in graphic writing, which not being beauty nor true inscape yet gives interest and makes ugliness even better than meaninglessness. On the Common the snow was channelled all in parallels by the sharp driving 365 wind and upon the tufts of grass (where by the dark colour shewing through it looked greyish) it came to turret-like clusters or like broken shafts of basalt.—In the Park in the afternoon the wind was driving little clouds of snow-dust which caught the sun as they rose and delightfully took the eyes: flying up 370 the slopes they looked like breaks of sunlight fallen through ravelled cloud upon the hills and again like deep flossy velvet blown to the root by breath which passed all along. Nearer at hand along the road it was gliding over the ground in white wisps that between trailing and flying shifted and wimpled 375 like so many silvery worms to and from one another.

May 14. Wych-elms not out till today.—The chestnuts down by St. Joseph's were a beautiful sight: each spike had its own pitch, yet each followed in its place in the sweep with a deeper and deeper stoop. When the wind tossed 380 them they plunged and crossed one another without losing their inscape. (Observe that motion multiplies inscape only when inscape is discovered, otherwise it disfigures)

May 18. Great brilliancy and projection: the eye seemed to fall perpendicular from level to level along our trees, the 385 nearer and further Park; all things hitting the sense with double but direct instress. . . .

This was later. One day when the bluebells were in bloom I wrote the following. I do not think I have ever seen anything more beautiful than the bluebell I have been looking at. I 390 know the beauty of our Lord by it. It[s inscape][1] is [mixed of] strength and grace, like an ash [tree]. The head is strongly drawn over [backwards] and arched down like a cutwater [drawing itself back from the line of the keel]. The lines of the bell strike and overlie this, rayed but not symmetrically, 395 some lie parallel. They look steely against [the] paper, the shades lying between the bells and behind the cockled petal-ends and nursing up the precision of their distinctness, the petal-ends themselves being delicately lit. Then there is the straightness of the trumpets in the bells softened by the slight 400 entasis and [by] the square splay of the mouth. One bell, the lowest, some way detached and carried on a longer footstalk, touched out with the tips of the petals an oval/ not like the rest in a plane perpendicular to the axis of the bell but a little atilt, 405 and so with [the] square-in-rounding turns of the petals. . . . There is a little drawing of this detached bell. It looks square-cut in the original 410

Aug. 25. This skeleton inscape of a spray-end of ash I broke at Wimbledon that summer is worth noticing for the suggested globe: it is leaf on the left and 415 keys on the right

Sept. 8. I took my vows.

[1] Hopkins's square brackets.

Sept. 9. To Stonyhurst to the seminary.

Sept. 24. First saw the Northern Lights. My eye was caught by beams of light and dark very like the crown of 420 horny rays the sun makes behind a cloud. At first I thought of silvery cloud until I saw that these were more luminous and did not dim the clearness of the stars in the Bear. They rose slightly radiating thrown out from the earthline. Then I saw soft pulses of light one after another rise and pass upwards 425 arched in shape but waveringly and with the arch broken. They seemed to float, not following the warp of the sphere as falling stars look to do but free though concentrical with it. This busy working of nature wholly independent of the earth and seeming to go on in a strain of time not reckoned 430 by our reckoning of days and years but simpler and as if correcting the preoccupation of the world by being pre-occupied with and appealing to and dated to the day of judgment was like a new witness to God and filled me with delightful fear   435

Oct. 20.—Laus Deo—the river today and yesterday. Yesterday it was a sallow glassy gold at Hodder Roughs and by watching hard the banks began to sail upstream, the scaping unfolded, the river was all in tumult but not running, only the lateral motions were perceived, and the curls of 440 froth where the waves overlap shaped and turned easily and idly.—I meant to have written more.—Today the river was wild, very full, glossy brown with mud, furrowed in permanent billows through which from head to head the water swung with a great foam. But at the Roughs the 445 sight was the burly water-backs which heave after heave kept tumbling up from the broken foam and their plump heap turning open in ropes of velvet

The winter was long and hard. I made many observations on freezing. For instance the crystals in mud.—Hailstones 450 are shaped like the cut of diamonds called brilliants.—I found one morning the ground in one corner of the garden full of small pieces of potsherd from which there rose up (and not dropped off) long icicles carried on in some way each like a forepitch of the shale of the piece of potsherd it 455 grew on, like a tooth to its root for instance, and most of them bended over and curled like so many tusks or horns or / best of all and what they looked likest when they first caught my eye / the first soft root-spurs thrown out from a sprouting chestnut. This bending of the icicle seemed so far 460 as I could see not merely a resultant, where the smaller spars of which it was made were still straight, but to have flushed them too.—The same day and others the garden mould very crisp and meshed over with a lace-work of needles leaving (they seemed) three-cornered openings: it 465 looked greyish and like a coat of gum on wood. Also the smaller crumbs and clods were lifted fairly up from the ground on upright ice-pillars, whether they had dropped these from themselves or drawn them from the soil: it was like a little Stonehenge—Looking down into the thick ice 470 of our pond I found the imprisoned air-bubbles nothing at random but starting from centres and in particular one most beautifully regular white brush of them, each spur of it a curving string of beaded and diminishing bubbles—The pond, I suppose from over pressure when it was less firm, was 475 mapped with a puzzle of very slight clefts branched with little sprigs: the pieces were odd-shaped and sized—though a square angular scaping could be just made out in the outline but the cracks ran deep through the ice markedly in planes and always the planes of the cleft on the surface. They 480 remained and in the end the ice broke up in just these pieces

[*1871*]

What you look hard at seems to look hard at you, hence

the true and the false instress of nature. One day early in
March when long streamers were rising from over Kemble 485
End one large flake loop-shaped, not a streamer but belonging to the string, moving too slowly to be seen, seemed to
cap and fill the zenith with a white shire of cloud. I looked
long up at it till the tall height and the beauty of the scaping
—regularly curled knots springing if I remember from fine 490
stems, like foliation in wood or stone—had strongly grown
on me. It changed beautiful changes, growing more into
ribs and one stretch of running into branching like coral.
Unless you refresh the mind from time to time you cannot
always remember or believe how deep the inscape in things is 495

End of March and beginning of April—This is the time
to study inscape in the spraying of trees, for the swelling buds
carry them to a pitch which the eye could not else gather—
for out of much much more, out of little not much, out of
nothing nothing: in these sprays at all events there is a new 500
world of inscape. The male ashes are very boldly jotted with the
heads of the bloom which tuft the outer ends of the branches.
The staff of each of these branches is closely knotted with the
places where buds are or have been, so that it is something
like a finger which has been tied up with string and keeps 505
the marks. They are in knops of a pair, one on each side, and
the knops are set alternately, at crosses with the knops above
and the knops below, the bud of course is a short smoke-black
pointed nail-head or beak pieced of four lids or nippers.
Below it, like the hollow below the eye or the piece between 510
the knuckle and the root of the nail, is a half-moon-shaped sill
as if once chipped from the wood and this gives the twig its
quaining in the outline. When the bud breaks at first it shews
a heap of fruity purplish anthers looking something like
unripe elder-berries but these push open into richly-branched 515
tree-pieces coloured buff and brown, shaking out loads of

pollen, and drawing the tuft as a whole into peaked quains—
mainly four, I think, two bigger and two smaller

Take a *few* primroses in a glass and the instress of—brilliancy, sort of starriness: I have not the right word—so simple   520
a flower gives is remarkable. It is, I think, due to the strong
swell given by the deeper yellow middle

'The young lambs bound As to the tabour's sound'.

They toss and toss: it is as if it were the earth that flung them,
not themselves. It is the pitch of graceful agility when we   525
think that.—April 16—Sometimes they rest a little space on
the hind legs and the forefeet drop curling in on the breast,
not so liquidly as we see it in the limbs of foals though

April 22. But such a lovely damasking in the sky as today
I never felt before. The blue was charged with simple instress,   530
the higher, zenith sky earnest and frowning, lower more
light and sweet. High up again, breathing through woolly
coats of cloud or on the quains and branches of the flying
pieces it was the true exchange of crimson, nearer the earth/
against the sun/ it was turquoise, and in the opposite south-   535
western bay below the sun it was like clear oil but just as full
of colour, shaken over with slanted flashing 'travellers', all
in flight, stepping one behind the other, their edges tossed
with bright ravelling, as if white napkins were thrown up
in the sun but not quite at the same moment so that they   540
were all in a scale down the air falling one after the other
to the ground

April 27. . . . Mesmerized a duck with chalk lines drawn
from her beak sometimes level and sometimes forwards on a
black table. They explain that the bird keeping the abiding   545
offscape of the hand grasping her neck fancies she is still
held down and cannot lift her head as long as she looks at the
chalk line, which she associates with the power that holds

her. This duck lifted her head at once when I put it down
on the table without chalk. But this seems inadequate. It is   550
most likely the fascinating instress of the straight white stroke

May 9. . . . This day and May 11 the bluebells in the little
wood between the College and the highroad and in one of the
Hurst Green cloughs. In the little wood/ opposite the light/
they stood in blackish spreads or sheddings like the spots on   555
a snake. The heads are then like thongs and solemn in grain
and grape-colour. But in the clough/ through the light/
they came in falls of sky-colour washing the brows and slacks
of the ground with vein-blue, thickening at the double,
vertical themselves and the young grass and brake fern   560
combed vertical, but the brake struck the upright of all
this with light winged transomes. It was a lovely sight.—
The bluebells in your hand baffle you with their inscape,
made to every sense: if you draw your fingers through
them they are lodged and struggle/ with a shock of wet   565
heads; the long stalks rub and click and flatten to a fan on
one another like your fingers themselves would when you
passed the palms hard across one another, making a brittle
rub and jostle like the noise of a hurdle strained by leaning
against; then there is the faint honey smell and in the mouth   570
the sweet gum when you bite them. But this is easy, it is the
eye they baffle. They give one a fancy of panpipes and of some
wind instrument with stops—a trombone perhaps. The
overhung necks—for growing they are little more than a
staff with a simple crook but in water, where they stiffen,   575
they take stronger turns, in the head like sheephooks or,
when more waved throughout, like the waves riding through
a whip that is being smacked—what with these overhung
necks and what with the crisped ruffled bells dropping mostly
on one side and the gloss these have at their footstalks they   580
have an air of the knights at chess. Then the knot or 'knoop'

of buds some shut, some just gaping, which makes the pencil of the whole spike, should be noticed: the inscape of the flower most finely carried out in the siding of the axes, each striking a greater and greater slant, is finished in these clus- 585 tered buds, which for the most part are not straightened but rise to the end like a tongue and this and their tapering and a little flattening they have make them look like the heads of snakes

May 17 etc.—I have several times seen the peacock with 590 train spread lately. It has a very regular warp, like a shell, in which the bird embays himself, the bulge being inwards below but the hollow inwards above, cooping him in and only opening towards the brim, where the feathers are beginning to rive apart. The eyes, which lie alternately when 595 the train is shut, like scales or gadroons, fall into irregular rows when it is opened, and then it thins and darkens against the light, it loses the moistness and satin it has when in the pack but takes another/ grave and expressive splendour, and the outermost eyes, detached and singled, give with 600 their corner fringes the suggestion of that inscape of the flowing cusped trefoil which is often effective in art. He shivers it when he first rears it and then again at intervals and when this happens the rest blurs and the eyes start forward.—I have thought it looks like a tray 605 or green basket or fresh-cut willow hurdle set all over with Paradise fruits cut through— first through a beard or golden fibre and then through wet flesh greener than greengages or purpler than grapes—or say that the knife had caught a tatter or flag of the 610 skin and laid it flat across the flesh—and then within all a sluggish corner drop of black or purple oil

June 13. A beautiful instance of inscape sided on the slide, that is/ successive sidings of one inscape, is seen in the

behaviour of the flag flower from the shut bud to the full 615
blowing: each term you can distinguish is beautiful in itself
and of course if the whole 'behaviour' were gathered up and
so stalled it would have a beauty of all the higher degree

June (*Later*). The Horned Violet is a pretty thing, gracefully
lashed. Even in withering the flower ran through beautiful 620
inscapes by the screwing up of the petals into straight little
barrels or tubes. It is not that inscape does not govern the
behaviour of things in slack and decay as one can see even
in the pining of the skin in the old and even in a skeleton but
that horror prepossesses the mind, but in this case there was 625
nothing in itself to shew even whether the flower were
shutting or opening

The 'pinion' of the blossom in the comfrey is remarkable for
the beauty of the coil and its regular lessening to its centre.
Perhaps the duller-coloured sorts shew it best   630

[*1872*]

March 13. After a time of trial and especially a morning
in which I did not know which way to turn as the account
of De Rancé's final conversion was being read at dinner the
verse *Qui confidunt in Domino sicut mons Sion* which satisfied 635
him and resolved him to enter his abbey of La Trappe by
the mercy of God came strongly home to me, too, so that I
was choked for a little while and could not keep in my tears

July 19. . . . Stepped into a barn of ours, a great shadowy
barn, where the hay had been stacked on either side, and 640
looking at the great rudely arched timberframes—principals(?)
and tie-beams, which make them look like bold big *A*'s with
the cross-bar high up—I thought how sadly beauty of inscape
was unknown and buried away from simple people and yet
how near at hand it was if they had eyes to see it and it could 645
be called out everywhere again. . . .

After the examinations we went for our holiday out to

Douglas in the Isle of Man Aug. 3. At this time I had first begun to get hold of the copy of Scotus on the Sentences in the Baddely library and was flush with a new stroke of enthusiasm. It may come to nothing or it may be a mercy from God. But just then when I took in any inscape of the sky or sea I thought of Scotus

Aug. 16. Big waves. There is a stack of rocks beyond the bay connected with the slope of the green banks by a neck of grass. Like an outwork or breaker to the stack is a long block consisting of a table or platform of even height sloping forward to the sea and flanked by two squarelike taller towers or shoulders, all shining when wet like smooth coal and cut and planed like masonry. The sea was breaking on all the stack and striking out all the ledges and edges at each breaker like snow does a building. In the narrow channel between this outwork and the main stack it was all a lather of foam, in which a spongy and featherlight brown scud bred from the churning of the water roped and changed, riding this and that, but never got clear of the channel. The overflow of the last wave came in from either side tilting up the channel and met halfway, each with its own moustache. When the wave ran very high it would brim over on the sloping shelf below me and move smoothly and steadily along it like the palm of a hand along a table drawing off the dust. In the channel I saw (as everywhere in surfy water) how the laps of foam mouthed upon one another. In watching the sea one should be alive to the oneness which all its motion and tumult receives from its perpetual balance and falling this way and that to its level

Dec. 12. A Blandyke. Hard frost, bright sun, a sky of blue 'water'. On the fells with Mr. Lucas. Parlick Pike and that ridge ruddy with fern and evening light. Ground sheeted with taut tattered streaks of crisp gritty snow. Green-white tufts of long bleached grass like heads of hair or the crowns of heads of hair, each a whorl of slender curves, one tuft taking up another—however these I might have noticed any day. I saw the inscape though freshly, as if my eye were still growing, though with a companion the eye and the ear are for the 685 most part shut and instress cannot come. We started pheasants and a grouse with flickering wings. On the slope of the far side under the trees the fern looked ginger-coloured over the snow. When there was no snow and dark greens about, as I saw it just over the stile at the top of the Forty-Acre 690 the other day, it made bats and splinters of smooth caky road-rut-colour

[*1873*]

April 8. The ashtree growing in the corner of the garden was felled. It was lopped first: I heard the sound and looking 695 out and seeing it maimed there came at that moment a great pang and I wished to die and not to see the inscapes of the world destroyed any more

May 11. Bluebells in Hodder wood, all hanging their heads one way. I caught as well as I could while my com- 700 panions talked the Greek rightness of their beauty, the lovely/ what people call/ 'gracious' bidding one to another or all one way, the level or stage or shire of colour they make hanging in the air a foot above the grass, and a notable glare the eye may abstract and sever from the blue colour/ 705 of light beating up from so many glassy heads, which like water is good to float their deeper instress in upon the mind

June 16. . . . As I passed the stables later and stayed to look at the peacocks John Myerscough came out to shew me a brood of little peafowl (though it could not be found at that time) 710 and the kindness touched my heart

I looked at the pigeons down in the kitchen yard and so on. They look like little gay jugs by shape when they walk,

strutting and jod-jodding with their heads. The two young
ones are all white and the pins of the folded wings, quill 715
pleated over quill, are like crisp and shapely cuttleshells found
on the shore. The others are dull thundercolour or black-
grape-colour except in the white pieings, the quills and tail,
and in the shot of the neck. I saw one up on the eaves of the
roof: as it moved its head a crush of satin green came and 720
went, a wet or soft flaming of the light

July 20. Water high at Hodder Roughs; where lit from
within looking like pale gold, elsewhere velvety brown
like ginger syrop; heavy locks or brushes like shaggy rope-
ends rolling from a corner of the falls and one huddling 725
over another; below the rock the bubble-jestled skirt of
foam jumping back against the fall, which cuts its way clean
and will not let it through, and there spitting up in long
white ragged shots and bushes like a mess of things of bramble,
and I saw by looking over nearer that those looping water- 730
springs that lace and dance and jockey in the air are strung
of single drops, the end one, like a tassel or a heavier bead,
the biggest; they look like bubbles in a quill. When the air
caught at the sill of the fall a sour yellow light flushed underneath like smoke kindling all along the rock, with a sullen 735
noise which we thought was thunder till someone pointed
out the cause, and this happened, I noticed, when one of the
bladders or blisters that form and come bumping to the top
in troubled water sailed over the falls

July 22. Very hot, though the wind, which was south, 740
dappled very sweetly on one's face and when I came out I
seemed to put it on like a gown as a man puts on the shadow
he walks into and hoods or hats himself with the shelter of a
roof, a penthouse, or a copse of trees, I mean it rippled and
fluttered like light linen, one could feel the folds and braids 745
of it—and indeed a floating flag is like wind visible and

what weeds are in a current; it gives it thew and fires it and bloods it in.—Thunderstorm in the evening, first booming in gong-sounds, as at Aosta, as if high up and so not reechoed from the hills; the lightning very slender and nimble and as if playing very near but after supper it was so bright and terrible some people said they had never seen its like. People were killed, but in other parts of the country it was more violent than with us. Flashes lacing two clouds above or the cloud and the earth started upon the eyes in live veins of rincing or riddling liquid white, inched and jagged as if it were the shivering of a bright riband string which had once been kept bound round a blade and danced back into its pleatings. Several strong thrills of light followed the flash but a grey smother of darkness blotted the eyes if they had seen the fork, also dull furry thickened scapes of it were left in them

Aug. 1. To Derby Castle at Douglas as last year

Aug. 16. We rose at four, when it was stormy and I saw dun-coloured waves leaving trailing hoods of white breaking on the beach. Before going I took a last look at the breakers, wanting to make out how the comb is morselled so fine into string and tassel, as I have lately noticed it to be. I saw big smooth flinty waves, carved and scuppled in shallow grooves, much swelling when the wind freshened, burst on the rocky spurs of the cliff at the little cove and break into bushes of foam. In an enclosure of rocks the peaks of the water romped and wandered and a light crown of tufty scum standing high on the surface kept slowly turning round: chips of it blew off and gadded about without weight in the air. At eight we sailed for Liverpool in wind and rain. I think it is the salt that makes rain at sea sting so much. There was a good-looking young man on board that got drunk and sung 'I want to go home to Mamma'. I did not look much at the sea: the crests I saw ravelled up by the wind into the air in arching

whips and straps of glassy spray and higher broken into 780
clouds of white and blown away. Under the curl shone a
bright juice of beautiful green. The foam exploding and
smouldering under water makes a chrysoprase green. From
Blackburn I walked: infinite stiles and sloppy fields, for there
has been much rain. A few big shining drops hit us aslant 785
as if they were blown off from eaves or leaves. Bright sunset:
all the sky hung with tall tossed clouds, in the west with
strong printing glass edges, westward lamping with tipsy
bufflight, the colour of yellow roses. Parlick ridge like a pale
goldish skin without body. The plain about Clitheroe was 790
sponged out by a tall white storm of rain. The sun itself and
the spot of 'session' dappled with big laps and flowers-in-
damask of cloud. But we hurried too fast and it knocked me
up. We went to the College, the seminary being wanted for
the secular priests' retreat: almost no gas, for the retorts are 795
being mended: therefore candles in bottles, things not ready,
darkness and despair. In fact being unwell I was quite down-
cast: nature in all her parcels and faculties gaped and fell
apart, *fatiscebat*, like a clod cleaving and holding only by
strings of root. But this must often be   800

　　Sept. 18. . . . I had a nightmare that night. I thought something or someone leapt onto me and held me quite fast: this
I think woke me, so that after this I shall have had the use of
reason. This first start is, I think, a nervous collapse of the same
sort as when one is very tired and holding oneself at stress 805
not to sleep yet/ suddenly goes slack and seems to fall and
wakes, only on a greater scale and with a loss of muscular control reaching more or less deep; this one to the chest and not
further, so that I could speak, whispering at first, then louder
—for the chest is the first and greatest centre of motion and 810
action, the seat of $\theta\upsilon\mu\acute{o}\varsigma$. I had lost all muscular stress
elsewhere but not sensitive, feeling where each limb lay and

thinking that I could recover myself if I could move my finger, I said, and then the arm and so the whole body. The feeling is terrible: the body no longer swayed as a piece by the 815 nervous and muscular instress seems to fall in and hang like a dead weight on the chest. I cried on the holy name and by degrees recovered myself as I thought to do. It made me think that this was how the souls in hell would be imprisoned in their bodies as in prisons and of what St. Theresa says of the 820 'little press in the wall' where she felt herself to be in her vision

[*1874*]

July 13. The comet—I have seen it at bedtime in the west, with head to the ground, white, a soft well-shaped tail, not big: I felt a certain awe and instress, a feeling of strange- 825 ness, flight (it hangs like a shuttlecock at the height, before it falls), and of threatening

July 23. To Beaumont: it was the rector's day. It was a lovely day: shires-long of pearled cloud under cloud, with a grey stroke underneath marking each row; beautiful 830 blushing yellow in the straw of the uncut ryefields, the wheat looking white and all the ears making a delicate and very true crisping along the top and with just enough air stirring for them to come and go gently; then there were fields reaping. All this I would have looked at again in returning but during 835 dinner I talked too freely and unkindly and had to do penance going home. One field I saw from the balcony of the house behind an elmtree, which it threw up, like a square of pale goldleaf, as it might be, catching the light

Our schools at Roehampton ended with two days of 840 examination before St. Ignatius' feast the 31st. I was very tired and seemed deeply cast down till I had some kind words from the Provincial. Altogether perhaps my heart has never been so burdened and cast down as this year. The tax on my strength has been greater than I have felt before: at least 845 now at Teignmouth I feel myself weak and can do little. But in all this our Lord goes His own way

Aug. 8. . . . near Bishopsteignton from a hilltop I looked into a lovely coomb that gave me the instress of *Weeping Winifred*, which all the west country seems to me to have: soft maroon or rosy cocoa-dust-coloured handkerchiefs of ploughfields, sometimes delicately combed with rows of green, their hedges bending in flowing outlines and now misted a little by the beginning of twilight ran down into it upon the shoulders of the hills; in the bottom crooked rows of rich tall elms, foreshortened by position, wound through it: some cornfields were still being carried

Aug. 17. We went over to Ugbrooke at Lord Clifford's invitation. . . . —I liked the family: all the children spoke in a very frank and simple way which shewed innocence as well as good breeding. As we drove home the stars came out thick: I leant back to look at them and my heart opening more than usual praised our Lord to and in whom all that beauty comes home

Sept. 6. With Wm. Kerr, who took me up a hill behind ours (ours is Mynefyr), a furze-grown and healthy hill, from which I could look round the whole country, up the valley towards Ruthin and down to the sea. The cleave in which Bodfari and Caerwys lie was close below. It was a leaden sky, braided or roped with cloud, and the earth in dead colours, grave but distinct. The heights by Snowdon were hidden by the clouds but not from distance or dimness. The nearer hills, the other side of the valley, shewed a hard and beautifully detached and glimmering brim against the light, which was lifting there. All the length of the valley the skyline of hills was flowingly written all along upon the sky. A blue bloom, a sort of meal, seemed to have spread upon the distant south, enclosed by a basin of hills. Looking all

round but most in looking far up the valley I felt an instress
and charm of Wales. Indeed in coming here I began to feel a   880
desire to do something for the conversion of Wales. I began
to learn Welsh too but not with very pure intentions perhaps.
However on consulting the Rector on this, the first day of
the retreat, he discouraged it unless it were purely for the sake
of labouring among the Welsh. Now it was not and so I saw I   885
must give it up. At the same time my music seemed to come
to an end. Yet, rather strangely, I had no sooner given up these
two things (which disappointed me and took an interest
away—and at that time I was very bitterly feeling the weariness of life and shed many tears, perhaps not wholly into the   890
breast of God but with some unmanliness in them too, and
sighed and panted to Him), I had no sooner given up the
Welsh than my desire seemed to be for the conversion of
Wales and I had it in mind to give up everything else for that;
nevertheless weighing this by St. Ignatius' rules of election I   895
decided not to do so

Sept. 20. Ordination of priests—sixteen, including many
Germans from Ditton. At the singing of the *Veni Creator* and
giving of the Orders I was by God's mercy deeply touched

Nov. 8. Walking with Wm. Splaine we saw a vast multi-   900
tude of starlings making an unspeakable jangle. They would
settle in a row of trees; then, one tree after another, rising
at a signal they looked like a cloud of specks of black snuff
or powder struck up from a brush or broom or shaken from
a wig; then they would sweep round in whirlwinds—you   905
could see the nearer and farther bow of the rings by the size
and blackness; many would be in one phase at once, all
narrow black flakes hurling round, then in another; then
they would fall upon a field and so on. . . . I thought they
must be full of enthusiasm and delight hearing their cries   910
and stirring and cheering one another

[*1875*]

Feb. 7. I asked Miss Jones in my Welsh lesson the Welsh for *fairy*, for we were translating Cinderella. She told me *cïpenăper* (or perhaps *cïpernăper, Anglice kippernapper*):[1] the word is nothing but *kidnapper*, moulded, according to their fashion, to give it a Welsh etymology, as she said, from *cïpio/* to snatch, to whisk away. However in coming to an understanding between ourselves what fairies (she says *fairess* by the way for a she-fairy) and kippernappers were, on my describing them as little people 'that high', she told me quite simply that she had seen them. It was on or near the Holywell road (she indicated the spot). She was going to her grandfather's farm on the hill, not far from where Justice Williams lived, on the slope of the Rhuallt. It was a busy time, haymaking I think. She was going up at five o'clock in the morning, when she saw three little boys of about four years old wearing little frock coats[2] and odd little caps running and dancing before her, taking hands and going round, then going further, still dancing and always coming together, she said. She would take no notice of them but went on to the house and there told them what she had seen and wondered that children could be out so early. 'Why she has seen the kippernappers' her grandmother said to her son, Susannah Jones' father. They were[3]

915
920
925
930
935

[1] She afterwards told me the true Welsh word *tolwyth-têg*. (Hopkins's note.)
[2] She afterwards called the coats long (*llaes*, that is/ trailing; perhaps unconfined by a girdle) and black. The caps or hats were round and black. (Hopkins's note.)
[3] [The extant Journal ends here.]

Comments on the Spiritual Exercises of St. Ignatius Loyola

On *Principium sive Fundamentum*

'Homo creatus est'—Aug. 20 1880: during this retreat, which I am making at Liverpool, I have been thinking about creation and this thought has led the way naturally through the exercises hitherto. I put down some thoughts.—We may learn that all things are created by consideration of the world without or of ourselves the world within. The former is the consideration commonly dwelt on, but the later takes on the mind more hold. I find myself both as man and as myself something most determined and distinctive, at pitch, more distinctive and higher pitched than anything else I see; I find myself with my pleasures and pains, my powers and my experiences, my deserts and guilt, my shame and sense of beauty, my dangers, hopes, fears, and all my fate, more important to myself than anything I see. And when I ask where does all this throng and stack of being, so rich, so distinctive, so important, come from/ nothing I see can answer me. And this whether I speak of human nature or of my individuality, my self being. For human nature, being more highly pitched, selved, and distinctive than anything in the world, can have been developed, evolved, condensed, from the vastness of the world not anyhow or by the working of common powers but only by one of finer or higher pitch and determination than itself and certainly than any that elsewhere we see, for this power had to force forward the starting or stubborn elements to the one pitch required. And this is much more true when we consider the mind; when I consider my selfbeing, my consciousness and feeling of myself, that taste of myself, of *I* and *me* above and in all things, which is more distinctive than the taste of ale or alum, more distinctive than the smell of walnutleaf or camphor, and is incommunicable by any means to another man (as when I was a child I used to ask myself: What must it be to be someone else?). Nothing else in nature comes near this unspeakable stress of pitch, distinctiveness, and selving, this selfbeing of my own. Nothing explains it or resembles it, except so far as this, that other men to themselves have the same feeling. But this only multiplies the phenomena to be explained so far as the cases are like and do resemble. But to me there is no resemblance: searching nature I taste *self* but at one tankard, that of my own being. The development, refinement, condensation of nothing shews any sign of being able to match this to me or give me another taste of it, a taste even resembling it.

One may dwell on this further. We say that any two things however unlike are in something like. This is the one exception: when I compare my self, my being-myself, with anything else whatever, all things alike, all in the same degree, rebuff me with blank unlikeness; so that my knowledge of it, which is so intense, is from itself alone, they in no way help me to understand it. And even those things with which I in some sort identify myself, as my country or family, and those things which I own and call mine, as my clothes and so on, all presuppose the stricter sense of *self* and *me* and *mine* and are from that derivative. . . .

SELECTIONS FROM LETTERS

1. To A. W. M. Baillie

July 10, 1863.

Dear Baillie,

Yes. You are a Fool.

I can shew it syllogistically, by an Epimediculum[1] or paradox- 5
ling. For you will allow that he who lies is a fool in the long
run, and that he who lies without any object to gain thereby
is immediately and directly a fool. Now you are not a fool.
But you say you are a fool. Therefore you lie. Syllogistically
then. 10

MAJOR PREMISS.

He who lies without an object to gain is a fool.

MINOR PREMISS.

You have lied without an object to gain.

CONCLUSION. 15

Therefore you are a fool.

Epimenidicularly[1] proved. However it contains two assump-
tions you might not perhaps allow me. . . .

I am sketching (in pencil chiefly) a good deal. I venture to
hope you will approve of some of the sketches in a Ruskinese 20
point of view:—if you do not, who will, my sole congenial
thinker on art? There are the most deliciously graceful
Giottesque ashes (should one say *ashs*?) here—I do not mean
Giottesque though, Peruginesque, Fra-Angelical(!), in
Raphael's earlier manner. I think I have told you that I 25
have particular periods of admiration for particular things
in Nature; for a certain time I am astonished at the beauty

[1] Thus in MS.

of a tree, shape, effect etc, then when the passion, so to speak, has subsided, it is consigned to my treasury of explored beauty, and acknowledged with admiration and interest 30 ever after, while something new takes its place in my enthusiasm. The present fury is the ash, and perhaps barley and two shapes of growth in leaves and one in tree boughs and also a conformation of fine-weather cloud. You remember the sketch that you would not criticize: I had continued it 35 to my satisfaction, when an insane fury induced me to ravage it—

None, I think, but an idiot could,—with a sky. It is now spoilt.

I will write again, and so please do you. 40

Believe me, dear Baillie, yours very sincerely,

GERARD M. HOPKINS

Manor Farm, Shanklin, Isle of Wight, July 13.

I think I could save my life by swimming on the river now.

My objection to the so-called Logical Mind rests finally on 45 the same ground as yours to General Rules.

2. To A. W. M. Baillie

Blunt House, Croydon, S.
Sept. 10, 1864.

Dear Baillie, . . . 50

I am meditating an essay, perhaps for the *Hexameron*, on some points of poetical criticism, and it is with reference to this a little that I have composed my thoughts on Tennyson. I think then the language of verse may be divided into three kinds. The first and highest is poetry proper, the language of 55 inspiration. The word inspiration need cause no difficulty. I mean by it a mood of great, abnormal in fact, mental acuteness, either energetic or receptive, according as the thoughts

which arise in it seem generated by a stress and action of the
brain, or to strike into it unasked. This mood arises from   60
various causes, physical generally, as good health or state
of the air or, prosaic as it is, length of time after a meal.
But I need not go into this; all that it is needful to mark is,
that the poetry of inspiration can only be written in this
mood of mind, even if it only last a minute, by poets them-   65
selves. Everybody of course has like moods, but not being
poets what they then produce is not poetry. The second
kind I call *Parnassian*. It can only be spoken by poets, but is
not in the highest sense poetry. It does not require the mood
of mind in which the poetry of inspiration is written. It is   70
spoken *on and from the level* of a poet's mind, not, as in the
other case, when the inspiration, which is the gift of genius,
raises him above himself. For I think it is the case with genius
that it is not when quiescent so very much above mediocrity
as the difference between the two might lead us to think, but   75
that it has the power and privilege of rising from that level
to a height utterly far from mediocrity: in other words that
its greatness is *that it can be* so great. You will understand.
Parnassian then is that language which genius speaks as
fitted to its exaltation, and place among other genius, but does   80
not sing (I have been betrayed into the whole hog of a
metaphor) in its flights. Great men, poets I mean, have each
their own dialect as it were of Parnassian, formed generally
as they go on writing, and at last,—that is the point to be
marked,—they can see things in this Parnassian way and   85
describe them in this Parnassian tongue, without further
effort of inspiration. In a poet's particular kind of Parnassian
lies most of his style, of his manner, of his mannerism if
you like. But I must not go farther without giving you
instances of Parnassian. I shall take one from Tennyson and   90
from *Enoch Arden*, from a passage much quoted already and

which will be no doubt often quoted, the description of
Enoch's tropical island.

> The mountain wooded to the peak, the lawns
> And winding glades high up like ways to Heaven,   95
> The slender coco's drooping crown of plumes,
> The lightning flash of insect and of bird,
> The lustre of the long convolvuluses
> That coil'd around the stately stems, and ran
> Ev'n to the limit of the land, the glows   100
> And glories of the broad belt of the world,
> All these he saw.

Now it is a mark of Parnassian that one could conceive
oneself writing it if one were the poet. Do not say that *if* you
were Shakespear you can imagine yourself writing Hamlet,   105
because that is just what I think you can*not* conceive. In a
fine piece of inspiration every beauty takes you as it were
by surprise, not of course that you did not think the writer
could be so great, for that is not it,—indeed I think it is a
mistake to speak of people admiring Shakespear more and   110
more as they live, for when the judgment is ripe and you
have read a good deal of any writer including his best things,
and carefully, then, I think, however high the place you give
him, that you must have rated him equally with his merits
however great they be; so that all after admiration cannot   115
increase but keep alive this estimate, make his greatness
stare into your eyes and din it into your ears, as it were, but
not make it greater,—but to go on with the broken sentence,
every fresh beauty could not in any way be predicted or
accounted for by what one has already read. But in Par-   120
nassian pieces you feel that if you were the poet you could
have gone on as he has done, you see yourself doing it, only
with the difference that if you actually try you find you

cannot write his Parnassian. Well now to turn to the piece
above. The glades being 'like ways to Heaven' is, I think,   125
a new thought, it is an inspiration. Not so the next line, that
is pure Parnassian. If you examine it the words are choice and
the description is beautiful and unexceptionable, but it does
not *touch* you. The next is more Parnassian still. In the next
lines I think the picture of the convolvuluses does touch;   130
but only the picture: the words are Parnassian. It is a very
good instance, for the lines are undoubtedly beautiful, but
yet I could scarcely point anywhere to anything more
idiomatically Parnassian, to anything which I more clearly
see myself writing *qua* Tennyson, than the words   135

The glows
And glories of the broad belt of the world.

What Parnassian is you will now understand, but I must
make some more remarks on it. I believe that when a poet
palls on us it is because of his Parnassian. We seem to have   140
found out his secret. Now in fact we have not found out more
than this, that when he is not inspired and in his flights, his
poetry does run in an intelligibly laid down path. Well,
it is notorious that Shakespear does not pall, and this is
because he uses, I believe, so little Parnassian. He does use   145
some, but little. Now judging from my own experience I
should say no author palls so much as Wordsworth; this is
because he writes such an 'intolerable deal of' Parnassian.

If with a critical eye and in a critical appreciative mood you
read a poem by an unknown author or an anonymous poem   150
by a known, but not at once recognizable, author, and he is
a real poet, then you will pronounce him so at once, and
the poem will seem truly inspired, though afterwards, when
you know the author, you will be able to distinguish his

inspirations from his Parnassian, and will perhaps think the 155
very piece which struck you so much at first mere Parnassian.
You know well how deadened, as it were, the critical faculties
become at times, when all good poetry alike loses its clear
ring and its charm; while in other moods they are so enlivened
that things that have long lost their freshness strike you with 160
their original definiteness and piquant beauty.

I think one had got into the way of thinking, or had not
got out of the way of thinking, that Tennyson was always
new, *touching*, beyond other poets, not pressed with human
ailments, never using Parnassian. So at least I used to think. 165
Now one sees he uses Parnassian; he is, one must see it, what
we used to call Tennysonian. But the discovery of this must
not make too much difference. When puzzled by one's doubts
it is well to turn to a passage like this. Surely your maturest
judgment will never be fooled out of saying that this is 170
divine, terribly beautiful—the stanza of *In Memoriam* beginning with the quatrain

> O Hesper o'er the buried sun,
>> And ready thou to die with him,
>> Thou watchest all things ever dim 175
> And dimmer, and a glory done.

I quote from memory. Inconsequent conclusion: Shakespear
is and must be utterly the greatest of poets.

Just to end what I was saying about poetry. There is a
higher sort of Parnassian which I call *Castalian*, or it may be 180
thought the lowest kind of inspiration. Beautiful poems
may be written wholly in it. Its peculiarity is that though
you can hardly conceive yourself having written in it, if in
the poet's place, yet it is too characteristic of the poet, too
so-and-so-all-over-ish, to be quite inspiration. 185

E.g.

> Yet despair
> Touches me not, though pensive as a bird
> Whose vernal coverts winter hath laid bare.

This is from Wordsworth, beautiful, but rather, too essentially Wordsworthian, too persistently his way of looking at things. The third kind is merely the language of verse as distinct from that of prose, Delphic, the tongue of the Sacred *Plain*, I may call it, used in common by poet and poetaster. Poetry when spoken is spoken in it, but to speak it is not necessarily to speak poetry. I may add there is also *Olympian*. This is the language of strange masculine genius which suddenly, as it were, forces its way into the domain of poetry, without naturally having a right there. Milman's poetry is of this kind I think, and Rossetti's *Blessed Damozel*. But unusual poetry has a tendency to seem so at first. . . .

You must be tired of Parnassian by this time. I must however add a few words left out. A great deal of Parnassian lowers a poet's average, and more than anything else lowers his fame I fear. This is in the main what is meant by artificial poetry; it is all Parnassian. When one reads Pope's Homer with a critical eye one sees, artificial as it is, in every couplet that he was a great man, but no doubt to an uncritical humour and an uncritical flippant modernist it does offer a great handle. . . .

3. To Robert Bridges

Stonyhurst, Whalley, Lancashire.
August 2, 1871.

My dear Bridges,

Our holidays have begun, so I will write again. I feel inclined to begin by asking whether you are secretary to the

International as you seem to mean me to think nothing too bad for you but then I remember that you never relished 'the intelligent artisan'. I must tell you I am always thinking of the Communist future. The too intelligent artisan is master of the situation I believe. Perhaps it is what everyone believes, I do not see the papers or hear strangers often enough to know. It is what Carlyle has long threatened and foretold. But his writings are, as he might himself say, 'most inefficacious-strenuous heaven-protestations, caterwaul, and Cassandra-wailings.' He preaches obedience but I do not think he has done much except to ridicule instead of strengthening the hands of the powers that be. Some years ago when he published his *Shooting Niagara* he did make some practical suggestions but so vague that they should rather be called '*too* dubious moonstone-grindings and on the whole imprac-ticable-practical unveracities'. However I am afraid some great revolution is not far off. Horrible to say, in a manner I am a Communist. Their ideal bating some things is nobler than that professed by any secular statesman I know of (I must own I live in bat-light and shoot at a venture). Besides it is just.—I do not mean the means of getting to it are. But it is a dreadful thing for the greatest and most necessary part of a very rich nation to live a hard life without dignity, know-ledge, comforts, delight, or hopes in the midst of plenty—which plenty they make. They profess that they do not care what they wreck and burn, the old civilization and order must be destroyed. This is a dreadful look out but what has the old civilization done for them? As it at present stands in England it is itself in great measure founded on wrecking. But they got none of the spoils, they came in for nothing but harm from it then and thereafter. England has grown hugely wealthy but this wealth has not reached the working classes; I expect it has made their condition worse. Besides this

LHS

iniquitous order the old civilization embodies another order
mostly old and what is new in direct entail from the old, the   250
old religion, learning, law, art, etc and all the history that
is preserved in standing monuments. But as the working
classes have not been educated they know next to nothing of
all this and cannot be expected to care if they destroy it. The
more I look the more black and deservedly black the future   255
looks, so I will write no more. . . .

Believe me your affectionate friend

GERARD HOPKINS, S.J.

4. To Robert Bridges

St. Beuno's, St. Asaph. Aug. 21, 1877   260

Dearest Bridges, . . .

I do not of course claim to have invented *sprung rhythms*
but only *sprung rhythm*; I mean that single lines and single
instances of it are not uncommon in English and I have
pointed them out in lecturing—e.g. 'why should this : desert   265
be?'—which the editors have variously amended; 'There to
meet : with Macbeth' or 'There to meet with Mac : beth';
Campbell has some throughout the *Battle of the Baltic*—'and
their fleet along the deep : proudly shone'—and *Ye Mariners*
—'as ye sweep : through the deep' etc; Moore has some   270
which I cannot recall; there is one in *Grongar Hill*; and,
not to speak of *Pom pom*, in Nursery Rhymes, Weather
Saws, and Refrains they are very common—but what I do
in the *Deutschland* etc is to enfranchise them as a regular
and permanent principle of scansion.   275

There are no outriding feet in the *Deutschland*. An outriding
foot is, by a sort of contradiction, a recognized extra-metrical
effect; it is and it is not part of the metre; not part of it, not

being counted, but part of it by producing a calculated effect which tells in the general success. But the long, e.g. seven- 280 syllabled, feet of the *Deutschland*, are strictly metrical. Out-riding feet belong to counterpointed verse, which supposes a well-known and unmistakable or unforgettable standard rhythm: the *Deutschland* is not counterpointed; counterpoint is excluded by sprung rhythm. But in some of my sonnets I 285 have mingled the two systems: this is the most delicate and difficult business of all.

The choruses in *Samson Agonistes* are intermediate between counterpointed and sprung rhythm. In reality they are sprung, but Milton keeps up a fiction of counterpointing the heard 290 rhythm (which is the same as the mounted rhythm) upon a standard rhythm which is never heard but only counted and therefore really does not exist. The want of a metrical notation and the fear of being thought to write mere rhythmic or (who knows what the critics might not have said?) even unrhythmic 295 prose drove him to this. Such rhythm as French and Welsh poetry has is sprung, counterpointed upon a counted rhythm, but it differs from Milton's in being little calculated, not more perhaps than prose consciously written rhythmically, like orations for instance; it is in fact the *native rhythm* of the 300 words used bodily imported into verse; whereas Milton's mounted rhythm is a real poetical rhythm, having its own laws and recurrence, but further embarrassed by having to count.

Why do I employ sprung rhythm at all? Because it is the 305 nearest to the rhythm of prose, that is the native and natural rhythm of speech, the least forced, the most rhetorical and emphatic of all possible rhythms, combining, as it seems to me, opposite and, one would have thought, incompatible excel-lences, markedness of rhythm—that is rhythm's self—and 310 naturalness of expression—for why, if it is forcible in prose to say 'lashed: rod', am I obliged to weaken this in verse, which ought to stronger, not weaker, into 'lashed birch-rod' or something?

My verse is less to be read than heard, as I have told you 315 before; it is oratorical, that is the rhythm is so. I think if you will study what I have here said you will be much more pleased with it and may I say? converted to it.

You ask may you call it 'presumptious jugglery'. No, but only for this reason, that *presumptious* is not English. 320

I cannot think of altering anything. Why should I? I do not write for the public. You are my public and I hope to convert you.

You say you would not for any money read my poem again. Nevertheless I beg you will. Besides money, you know, there 325 is love. If it is obscure do not bother yourself with the meaning but pay attention to the best and most intelligible stanzas, as the two last of each part and the narrative of the wreck. If you had done this you would have liked it better and sent me some serviceable criticisms, but now your criticism is of no 330 use, being only a protest memorializing me against my whole policy and proceedings.

I may add for your greater interest and edification that what refers to myself in the poem is all strictly and literally true and did all occur; nothing is added for poetical padding. 335

Believe me your affectionate friend

GERARD M. HOPKINS, S.J.

5. To Robert Bridges

Stonyhurst College, Blackburn (or Whalley).
May 13, 1878. 340

Dearest Bridges, . . .

I enclose you my Eurydice, which the *Month* refused. It is

my only copy. Write no bilgewater about it: I will presently
tell you what that is and till then excuse the term. I must tell
you I am sorry you never read the Deutschland again.   345

Granted that it needs study and is obscure, for indeed I was
not over-desirous that the meaning of all should be quite
clear, at least unmistakeable, you might, without the effort
that to make it all out would seem to have required, have
nevertheless read it so that lines and stanzas should be left in 350
the memory and superficial impressions deepened, and have
liked some without exhausting all. I am sure I have read and
enjoyed pages of poetry that way. Why, sometimes one
enjoys and admires the very lines one cannot understand, as
for instance 'If it were done when 'tis done' sqq., which is all 355
obscure and disputed, though how fine it is everybody sees
and nobody disputes. And so of many more passages in
Shakespere and others. Besides you would have got more
weathered to the style and its features—not really odd. Now
they say that vessels sailing from the port of London will 360
take (perhaps it should be/ used once to take) Thames water
for the voyage: it was foul and stunk at first as the ship
worked but by degrees casting its filth was in a few days very
pure and sweet and wholesomer and better than any water in
the world. However that maybe, it is true to my purpose. 365
When a new thing, such as my ventures in the Deutschland
are, is presented us our first criticisms are not our truest, best,
most homefelt, or most lasting but what come easiest on the
instant. They are barbarous and like what the ignorant and
the ruck say. This was so with you. The Deutschland on 370
her first run worked very much and unsettled you, thickening
and clouding your mind with vulgar mud-bottom and
common sewage (I see that I am going it with the image) and
just then unhappily *you drew* off your criticisms all stinking
(a necessity now of the image) and bilgy, whereas if you 375

had let your thoughts cast themselves they would have been clearer in themselves and more to my taste too. I did not heed them therefore, perceiving they were a first drawing-off. Same of the Eurydice—which being short and easy please read more than once. . . Your bodysnatch story is ghastly, 380 but so are all bodysnatch stories. My grandfather was a surgeon, a fellow-student of Keats', and once conveyed a body through Plymouth at the risk of his own.

Believe me your affectionate friend

GERARD M. HOPKINS, S.J. 385

May 21, 1878. . . . To do the Eurydice any kind of justice you must not slovenly read it with the eyes but with your ears, as if the paper were declaiming it at you. For instance the line 'she had come from a cruise training seamen' read without stress and declaim is mere Lloyd's Shipping Intelli- 390 gence; properly read it is quite a different thing. Stress is the life of it.

6. To R. W. Dixon

111 Mount Street, Grosvenor Square, W.
Oct. 5, 1878.   395

Very Reverend and Dear Sir, . . .

You ask, do I write verse myself. What I had written I burnt before I became a Jesuit and resolved to write no more, as not belonging to my profession, unless it were by the wish of my superiors; so for seven years I wrote nothing but two or 400 three little presentation pieces which occasion called for. But when in the winter of '75 the Deutschland was wrecked in the mouth of the Thames and five Franciscan nuns, exiles from Germany by the Falck Laws, aboard of her were drowned I was affected by the account and happening to say 405

so to my rector he said that he wished someone would write
a poem on the subject. On this hint I set to work and, though
my hand was out at first, produced one. I had long had
haunting my ear the echo of a new rhythm which now I
realized on paper. To speak shortly, it consists in scanning by 410
accents or stresses alone, without any account of the number
of syllables, so that a foot may be one strong syllable or it may
be many light and one strong. I do not say the idea is altogether new; there are hints of it in music, in nursery rhymes
and popular jingles, in the poets themselves, and, since 415
then, I have seen it talked about as a thing possible in critics.
Here are instances—'*Díng, dóng, béll* Pússy's ín the wéll; *Whó
pút* her ín? Líttle Jóhnny Thin. *Whó púlled* her óut? Líttle
Jóhnny Stóut.' For if each line has three stresses or three feet
it follows that some of the feet are of one syllable only. So 420
too '*Óne, twó,* Búckle my shóe' *passim.* In Campbell you have
'Ánd their fléet alóng the *déep próudly* shóne'—'Ít was tén of
Ápril *mórn bý* the chíme' etc; in Shakespere 'Who shd. *this*
désert bé?' corrected wrongly by the editors; in Moore a little
melody I cannot quote; etc. But no one has professedly used 425
it and made it the principle throughout, that I know of.
Nevertheless to me it appears, I own, to be a better and more
natural principle than the ordinary system, much more
flexible, and capable of much greater effects. However I had
to mark the stresses in blue chalk, and this and my rhymes 430
carried on from one line into another and certain chimes
suggested by the Welsh poetry I had been reading (what
they call *cyng-hanedd*) and a great many more oddnesses
could not but dismay an editor's eye, so that when I offered
it to our magazine the *Month*, though at first they accepted 435
it, after a time they withdrew and dared not print it. After
writing this I held myself free to compose, but cannot find
it in my conscience to spend time upon it; so I have done

little and shall do less. But I wrote a shorter piece on the
Eurydice, also in 'sprung rhythm', as I call it, but simpler,   440
shorter, and without marks, and offered the *Month* that
too, but they did not like it either. Also I have written some
sonnets and a few other little things; some in sprung rhythm,
with various other experiments—as 'outriding feet', that is
parts of which do not count in the scanning (such as you   445
find in Shakespere's later plays, but as a licence, whereas
mine are rather calculated effects); others in the ordinary
scanning *counterpointed* (this is counterpoint: '*Hóme* to his
móther's hóuse *prívate* retúrned' and '*Bút to vánquish* by wisdom héllish wíles' etc); others, one or two, in common   450
uncounterpointed rhythm. But even the impulse to write
is wanting, for I have no thought of publishing.

I should add that Milton is the great standard in the use of
counterpoint. In *Paradise Lost* and *Regained*, in the last more
freely, it being an advance in his art, he employs counter-   455
point more or less everywhere, markedly now and then;
but the choruses of *Samson Agonistes* are in my judgment
counterpointed throughout; that is, each line (or nearly so)
has two different coexisting scansions. But when you reach
that point the secondary or 'mounted rhythm', which is neces-   460
sarily a sprung rhythm, overpowers the original or conventional one and then this becomes superfluous and may be
got rid of; by taking that last step you reach simple sprung
rhythm. Milton must have known this but had reasons for
not taking it. . . .   465

Believe me, dear Sir, very sincerely yours

GERARD HOPKINS

7. To R. W. Dixon

St. Aloysius' Presbytery, St. Giles's, Oxford.
Feb. 27, 1879.   470

Very Reverend and Dear Sir, . . .

Marvel, of whom I have only read extracts, is a most
rich and nervous poet. Thomas[1] Vaughan's poems were
reprinted not so long ago. He was a follower of Herbert
both in life and style: he was in fact converted from worldly   475
courses by reading Herbert's poems on a sickbed and even
his muse underwent a conversion (for he had written before).
He has more glow and freedom than Herbert but less fragrant
sweetness. Somewhere he speaks of some spot 'primrosed
and hung with shade' and one piece ends   480

And here in dust and dirt, O here
The lilies of his love appear.

(I am assuming that you have not got the book.) Still I do
not think him Herbert's equal.

You call Tennyson 'a great outsider'; you mean, I think, to   485
the soul of poetry. I feel what you mean, though it grieves me
to hear him depreciated, as of late years has often been
done. Come what may he will be one of our greatest poets.
To me his poetry appears 'chryselephantine'; always of
precious mental material and each verse a work of art, no   490
botchy places, not only so but no half wrought or low-toned
ones, no drab, no brown-holland; but the form, though fine,
not the perfect artist's form, not equal to the material.
When the inspiration is genuine, arising from personal
feeling, as in *In Memoriam*, a divine work, he is at his best   495
or when he is rhyming pure and simple imagination, without

[1] A slip for Henry.

afterthought, as in the *Lady of Shalott*, *Sir Galahad*, the *Dream of Fair Women*, or *Palace of Art*. But the want of perfect form in the imagination comes damagingly out when he undertakes longer works of fancy, as his Idylls: they are unreal 500 in motive and incorrect, uncanonical so to say, in detail and keepings. He should have called them *Charades from the Middle Ages* (dedicated by permission to H. R. H. etc). The Galahad of one of the later ones is quite a fantastic charade-playing trumpery Galahad, merely playing the fool over Christian 505 heroism. Each scene is a triumph of language and of bright picturesque, but just like a charade—where real lace and good silks and real jewelry are used, because the actors are private persons and wealthy, but it is acting all the same and not only so but the make-up has less pretence of correct 510 keeping than at Drury Lane. His opinions too are not original, often not independent even, and they sink into vulgarity: not only *Locksley Hall* but *Maud* is an ungentlemanly row and *Aylmer's Field* is an ungentlemanly row and the *Princess* is an ungentlemanly row. To be sure this gives him vogue, 515 popularity, but not that sort of ascendancy Goethe had or even Burns, scoundrel as the first was, not to say the second; but then they spoke out the real human rakishness of their hearts and everybody recognized the really beating, though rascal, vein. And in his rhetorical pieces he is at his worst, 520 as the *Lord of Burleigh* and *Lady Clare Vere de Vere* (downright haberdasher). But for all this he is a glorious poet and all he does is chryselephantine. Though by the by I owe him a grudge for *Queen Mary*, written to please the mob, and for that other drama where a portent of a man in flaxen locks 525 and ring-mail mouths rationalism 'to torment us before the time'. . . .

Believe me your sincere friend

GERARD M. HOPKINS, S.J.

8. To Robert Bridges   530

Catholic Church, St. Giles's, Oxford.
April 22, 1879.

Dearest Bridges, . . .

I think I have seen nothing of Lang's but in some magazine;
also a sonnet prefixed to his translation of the Odyssey. I   535
liked what I read, but not so that it left a deep impression.
It is in the Swinburnian kind, is it not? (I do not think that
kind goes far: it expresses passion but not feeling, much less
character. This I say in general or of Swinburne in particular.
Swinburne's genius is astonishing, but it will, I think, only   540
do one thing.) Everybody cannot be expected to like my
pieces. Moreover the oddness may make them repulsive at
first and yet Lang might have liked them on a second reading.
Indeed when, on somebody returning me the *Eurydice*, I
opened and read some lines, reading, as one commonly reads   545
whether prose or verse, with the eyes, so to say, only, it struck
me aghast with a kind of raw nakedness and unmitigated
violence I was unprepared for: but take breath and read it
with the ears, as I always wish to be read, and my verse
becomes all right. I do warm to that good Mr. Gosse for   550
liking and, you say, 'taking' my pieces: I may then have
contributed fuel to his Habitual Joy. . . .

Your affectionate friend

GERARD M. HOPKINS, S.J.

9. To R. W. Dixon　　　555

Manresa House, Roehampton, London, S.W.
(By the by have you read Lothair? because
this house is the divine Theodora's: some of
the scenes are laid here.)

　　　　Oct. 12, 1881.　　　560

My Dear Friend, ...

In speaking of 'frigid fancy' I referred to the particular
passage only. But Browning has, I think, many frigidities.
Any untruth to nature, to human nature, is frigid. Now
he has got a great deal of what came in with Kingsley and　565
the Broad Church school, a way of talking (and making his
people talk) with the air and spirit of a man bouncing up from
table with his mouth full of bread and cheese and saying that
he meant to stand no blasted nonsense. There is a whole
volume of Kingsley's essays which is all a kind of munch and a　570
not standing of any blasted nonsense from cover to cover. Do
you know what I mean? The *Flight of the Duchess*, with the
repetition of 'My friend', is in this vein. Now this is *one* mood
or vein of human nature, but they would have it all and
look at all human nature through it. And Tennyson in his　575
later works has been 'carried away with their dissimulation.'
The effect of this style is a frigid bluster. A true humanity
of spirit, neither mawkish on the one hand nor blustering on
the other, is the most precious of all qualities in style, and this
I prize in your poems, as I do in Bridges'. After all it is the　580
breadth of his human nature that we admire in Shakespeare.

I read some, not much, of the *Ring and the Book*, but as the
tale was not edifying and one of our people, who had been
reviewing it, said that further on it was coarser, I did not see,
without a particular object, sufficient reason for going on　585

with it. So far as I read I was greatly struck with the skill in which he displayed the facts from different points of view: this is masterly, and to do it through three volumes more shews a great body of genius. I remember a good case of 'the impotent collection of particulars' of which you speak in the 590 description of the market place at Florence where he found the book of the trial: it is a pointless photograph of still life, such as I remember in Balzac, minute upholstery description; only that in Balzac, who besides is writing prose, all tells and is given with a reserve and simplicity of style which Browning 595 has not got. Indeed I hold with the oldfashioned criticism that Browning is not really a poet, that he has all the gifts but the one needful and the pearls without the string; rather one should say raw nuggets and rough diamonds. I suppose him to resemble Ben Jonson, only that Ben Jonson has more 600 real poetry. . . .

Believe me your affectionate friend

GERARD M. HOPKINS, S.J.

10. To Coventry Patmore

University College, Stephen's Green, Dublin. 605
Oct. 6, 1886.

My Dear Mr. Patmore,—I have just returned from a very reviving fortnight or so of North Wales, the true Arcadia of wild beauty. . . .

You are not to think I now begin to admire Barnes: I 610 always did so, but it was long since I had read him. (Bridges is quite wrong about him and off his orthodoxy.) I scarcely understand you about reflected light: every true poet, I thought, must be original and originality a condition of poetic

genius; so that each poet is like a species in nature (*not* an   615
individuum genericum or *specificum*) and can never recur. That
nothing should be old or borrowed however cannot be, and
that I am sure you never meant.

Still I grant in Barnes an unusual independence and originality, due partly to his circumstances. It is his naturalness that   620
strikes me most; he is like an embodiment or incarnation or
manmuse of the country, of Dorset, of rustic life and
humanity. He comes, like Homer and all poets of native epic,
provided with epithets, images, and so on which seem to
have been tested and digested for a long age in their native   625
air and circumstances and to have a *keeping* which nothing
else could give; but in fact they are rather all of his own
finding and first throwing off. This seems to me very high
praise. It is true they are not far-fetched or exquisite (I mean
for instance his mentions of rooks or of brooks) but they are   630
straight from nature and quite fresh. His rhythms are charm-
ing and most characteristic: these too smack of the soil. However his employment of the Welsh *cynghanedd* or chime
I do not look on as quite successful. To tell the truth, I think
I could do that better, and it is an artificial thing and not   635
much in his line. I mean like *Paladore* and *Polly dear*, which is
in my judgment more of a miss than a hit.) I have set tunes
to two of them which appear to me very suitable to the
words and as if drawn out of them, and one I have har-
monised and got today played; but I can never succeed   640
with piano music, for the piano cannot really execute independent parts, as I make mine; indeed my pianist said to me,
Your music dates from a time before the piano was invented.
However two schoolboys sang the air; which went well.
But now no more of Barnes or of music, for I have over-   645
hanging me 500 examination papers and that only one batch
out of three.

With the kindest remembrances to Mrs. Patmore and the Miss Patmores, I am your sincere friend

GERARD M. HOPKINS, S.J. 650

Before I went to Wales I was much pulled down: that was why I did not sooner write. Bridges says Barnes has no fire, and this I think we must grant.

11. To R. W. Dixon

University College, St. Stephen's Green, Dublin. 655
Oct. 23, 1886.

My dear Friend, . . .

I feel now I am warm and my hand is in for my greater task, Wordsworth's ode; and here, my dear friend, I must earnestly remonstrate with you; must have it out with you. Is 660 it possible that—but it is in black and white: you say the ode is not, for Wordsworth, good; and much less great.

To say it was the second ode in the language was after all only a comparative remark: one might maintain, though I daresay you will not, that English is not rich in odes. The 665 remark therefore is not of itself extravagant. But if the speaker had said that it was one of the dozen or of the half dozen finest odes of the world I must own that to me there would have seemed no extravagance. There have been in all history a few, a very few men, whom common repute, even 670 where it did not trust them, has treated as having had something happen to them that does not happen to other men, as having *seen something*, whatever that really was. Plato is the most famous of these. Or to put it as it seems to me I must somewhere have written to you or to somebody, human 675 nature in these men saw something, got a shock; wavers in opinion, looking back, whether there was anything in it or no; but is in a tremble ever since. Now what Wordsworthians mean is, what would seem to be the growing mind of the English speaking world and may perhaps come to be that of 680 the world at large/ is that in Wordsworth when he wrote that ode human nature got another of those shocks, and the tremble from it is spreading. This opinion I do strongly share; I am, ever since I knew the ode, in that tremble. You know what happened to crazy Blake, himself a most poetically 685 electrical subject both active and passive, at his first hearing: when the reader came to 'The pansy at my feet' he fell into a hysterical excitement. Now commonsense forbid we should take on like these unstrung hysterical creatures: still it was a proof of the power of the shock. 690

The ode itself seems to me better than anything else I know of Wordsworth's, so much as to equal or outweigh everything else he wrote: to me it appears so. For Wordsworth was an imperfect artist, as you say: as his matter varied in importance and as he varied in insight (for he had 695 a profound insight of some things and little of others) so does the value of his work vary. Now the interest and importance of the matter were here of the highest, his insight was at its very deepest, and hence to my mind the extreme value of the poem. 700

His powers rose, I hold, with the subject: the execution is so fine. The rhymes are so musically interlaced, the rhythms so happily succeed (surely it is a magical change 'O joy that in our embers'), the diction throughout is so charged and steeped in beauty and yearning (what a stroke 'The moon 705 doth with delight'!). It is not a bit of good my going on if, which is to me so strange in you and disconcerting, you do not feel anything of this. But I do hope you will reconsider it. For my part I should think St. George and St. Thomas of Canterbury wore roses in heaven for England's sake on the 710

day that ode, not without their intercession, was penned;
for, to better a little the good humoured old cynical proverb,
'When grace of God is gone and spent Then learning is most
excellent' and goes to make the greatness of a nation—
which is what I urge on Bridges and now on you, to get   715
yourselves known and be up betimes on our Parnassus.

Now no more. I will copy you soon some odd ends,
sonnets. Have you my song for my play of *St. Winefred*
called *The Leaden Echo and the Golden Echo*? If not I will
try and copy it as times serves: I never did anything more   720
musical. May the Muses bring you to a better mind. May
God Almighty, and this without reserve. I am your affectionate friend
GERARD M. HOPKINS, S.J.

Oct. 24. Examinations over and I begin lecturing tomorrow.   725

12. To Coventry Patmore

University College, St. Stephen's Green, Dublin.
Oct. 20, 1887.

My Dear Mr. Patmore, . . .

During the summer examinations one of my colleagues   730
brought in one day a *St. James's Gazette* with a piece of
criticism he said it was a rare pleasure to read. It proved to
be a review by you of Colvin's book on Keats. Still, enlight-
ening as the review was, I did not think it really just. You
classed Keats with the feminine geniuses among men and   735
you would have it that he was not the likest but rather the
unlikest of our poets to Shakspere. His poems, I know, are
very sensuous and indeed they are sensual. This sensuality is
their fault, but I do not see that it makes them feminine. But
at any rate (and the second point includes the first) in this   740
fault he resembles, not differs from Shakspere. For Keats died

MHS

very young and we have only the work of his first youth.
Now if we compare that with Shakspere's early work,
written at an age considerably more than Keats's, was it not?
such as *Venus and Adonis* and *Lucrece*, it is, as far as the work of 745
two very original minds ever can be, greatly like in its
virtues and its vices; more like, I do think, than that of any
writer you could quote after the Elizabethan age; which
is what the common opinion asserts. It may be that Keats
was no dramatist (his *Otho* I have not seen); but it is not for 750
that, I think, that people have made the comparison. The *Cap
and Bells* is an unhappy performance, so bad that I could not
get through it; senselessly planned to have no plan and
doomed to fail: but Keats would have found out that. He was
young; his genius intense in its quality; his feeling for 755
beauty, for perfection intense; he had found his way right
in his Odes; he would find his way right at last to the true
functions of his mind. And he was at a great disadvantage
in point of education compared with Shakespere. Their
classical attainments may have been much of a muchness, 760
but Shakespere had the school of his age. It was the Renais-
sance: the ancient Classics were deeply and enthusiastically
studied and influenced directly or indirectly all, and the new
learning had entered into a fleeting but brilliant combination
with the medieval tradition. All then used the same forms 765
and keepings. But in Keats's time, and worst in England,
there was no one school; but experiment, division, and
uncertainty. He was one of the beginners of the Romantic
movement, with the extravagance and ignorance of
his youth. After all is there anything in *Endymion* worse than 770
the passage in *Romeo and Juliet* about the County Paris as a
book of love that must be bound and I can't tell what? It
has some kind of fantastic beauty, like an arabesque; but in
the main it is nonsense. And about the true masculine fibre

in Keats's mind Matthew Arnold has written something 775
good lately. . . .

Believe me very sincerely yours

GERARD M. HOPKINS

13. To Robert Bridges

University College, St. Stephen's Green, Dublin. 780
Nov. 6, 1887.

Dearest Bridges, . . .

No, I do not ask 'enthusiastic praise'. But is it not the case
that the day when you could give enthusiastic praise to
anything is passing or past? As for modern novels I will only 785
say one thing now. It is in modern novels that wordpainting
most abounds and now the fashion is to be so very subtle and
advanced as to despise wordpainting and to say that old
masters were not wordpainters. Just so. Wordpainting is, in
the verbal arts, the great success of our day. Every age in art 790
has its secret and its success, where even second rate men are
masters. Second rate, third rate men are fine designers in
Japan; second rate men were masters of painting in Raphael's
time; second rate men were masters of sculpture in Phidias'
time; second rate men of oratory in Cicero's; and so of many 795
things. These successes are due to steady practice, to the continued action of a school: one man cannot compass them. And
wordpainting is in our age a real mastery and the second rate
men of this age often beat at it the first rate of past ages. And
this I shall not be bullied out of.   800

For my case I should also remark that we turned up a difference of taste and judgment, if you remember, about Dryden. I
can scarcely think of you not admiring Dryden without, I may
say, exasperation And my style tends always more towards

Dryden. What is there in Dryden? Much, but above all this: 805
he is the most masculine of our poets; his style and his
rhythms lay the strongest stress of all our literature on the
naked thew and sinew of the English language, the praise that
with certain qualifications one would give in Greek to Demos-
thenes, to be the greatest master of bare Greek. I am driven to   810
the blackguard device of a palimpsest envelope.

14. To Coventry Patmore

Milltown Park, Milltown, Dublin.
May 6, 1888.

My Dear Mr. Patmore, . . .   815

Since I last wrote I have reread Keats a little and the force
of your criticism on him has struck me more than it did. It is
impossible not to feel with weariness how his verse is at every
turn abandoning itself to an unmanly and enervating luxury.
It appears too that he said something like 'O for a life of   820
impressions instead of thoughts!' It was, I suppose, the life he
tried to lead. The impressions are not likely to have been all
innocent and they soon ceased in death. His contemporaries
as Wordsworth, Byron, Shelley, and even Leigh Hunt, right
or wrong, still concerned themselves with great causes, as   825
liberty and religion; but he lived in mythology and fairyland
the life of a dreamer. Nevertheless I feel and see in him the
beginnings of something opposite to this, of an interest in
higher things and of powerful and active thought. On this
point you should if possible read what Matthew Arnold wrote.   830
His mind had, as it seems to me, the distinctively masculine
powers in abundance, his character the manly virtues, but
while he gave himself up to dreaming and self indulgence of
course they were in abeyance. Nor do I mean that he would

have turned to a life of virtue—only God can know that—, 835
but that his genius would have taken to an austerer utterance
in art. Reason, thought, what he did not want to live by,
would have asserted itself presently and perhaps have been
as much more powerful than that of his contemporaries as his
sensibility or impressionableness, by which he did want to 840
live, was keener and richer than theirs. His defects were due to
youth—the self indulgence of his youth; its ill-education;
and also, as it seems to me, to its breadth and pregnancy,
which, by virtue of a fine judgment already able to restrain
but unable to direct, kept him from flinging himself blindly 845
on the specious Liberal stuff that crazed Shelley and indeed,
in their youth, Wordsworth and Coleridge. His mind played
over life as a whole, so far as he a boy, without (seemingly)
a dramatic but still with a deeply observant turn and also
without any noble motive, felt at first hand, impelling 850
him to look below its surface, could at that time see it. He was,
in my opinion, made to be a thinker, a critic, as much as a
singer or artist of words. This can be seen in certain reflective
passages, as the opening to *Endymion* and others in his poems.
These passages are the thoughts of a mind very ill instructed 855
and in opposition; keenly sensible of wrongness in things
established but unprovided with the principles to correct
that by. Both his principles of art and his practice were in
many things vicious, but he was correcting them, even
eagerly; for *Lamia* one of his last works shews a deliberate 860
change in manner from the style of *Endymion* and in fact goes
too far in change and sacrifices things that had better have
been kept. Of construction he knew nothing to the last: in
this same *Lamia* he has a long introduction about Mercury,
who is only brought in to disenchant Lamia and ought not 865
to have been employed or else ought to be employed again.
The story has a moral element or interest; Keats was aware

of this and touches on it at times, but could make nothing of it; in fact the situation at the end is that the sage Apollonius does more harm than the witch herself had done—kills the hero; and Keats does not see that this implies one of two things, either some lesson of the terrible malice of evil which when it is checked drags down innocence in its own ruin or else the exposure of Pharisaic pretence in the wouldbe moralist. But then if I could have said this to Keats I feel sure he would have seen it. In due time he would have seen these thing himself. Even when he is misconstructing one can remark certain instinctive turns of construction in his style, shewing his latent power—for instance the way the vision is introduced in *Isabella*. Far too much now of Keats. . . .

Yours very sincerely

GERARD M. HOPKINS

15. To Robert Bridges

University College,
St. Stephen's Green, Dublin.
Sept. 25, 1888.

Dearest Bridges,

I am sorry to hear of our differing so much in taste: I was hardly aware of it. (It is not nearly so sad as differing in religion). I feel how great the loss is of not reading, as you say; but if I did read I do not much think the effect of it would be what you seem to expect, on either my compositions or my judgments.

I *must* read something of Greek and Latin letters and lately I sent you a sonnet, on the Heraclitean Fire, in which a great deal of early Greek philosophical thought was distilled; but the liquor of the distillation did not taste very Greek, did it? The effect of studying masterpieces is to make me admire and do otherwise. So it must be on every original artist to some degree, on me to a marked degree. Perhaps then more reading 900 would only *refine my singularity*, which is not what you want....

But not on my criticisms either, I suspect. Wide reading does two things—it extends knowledge and it adjusts the judgment. Now it is mostly found that a learned judgment is less singular than an unlearned one and oftener agrees with 905 the common and popular judgment, with which it coincides as a fine balance or other measure does with the rule of thumb. But, so far as I see, where we differ in judgment, my judgments are less singular than yours; I agree more than you do with the mob and with the *communis criticorum*. 910 Presumably I should agree with these still more if I read more and so differ still more from you than now. Who for instance is singular about Dryden, you or I? These considerations are very general, but so far as they go they appear to be reasonable. 915

To return to composition for a moment: what I want there, to be more intelligible, smoother, and less singular, is an audience. I think the fragments I wrote of *St. Winefred*, which was meant to be played, were not hard to understand. My prose I am sure is clear and even flowing. This reminds me 920 that I have written a paper for an Irish magazine the *Lyceum*, organ of this College, one may say. I was asked and I rewrote something I had by me and it is to appear next month. And yet I bet you it will not: my luck will not allow it. But if it does, I then bet you it is intelligible, though on an obstruse 925 subject, Statistics and Free Will—and I mean very intelligible. (This, by the bye, is a badly made logical bed; for I can only win one wager by losing the other. But never mind.)

I send an improved version of my war-song, less open to the objections made, and am your affectionate friend 930

GERARD HOPKINS

NOTES TO THE VERSE

PAGE 37. WINTER WITH THE GULF STREAM. (?) Hampstead, 1862. Published in *Once a Week*, 14 Feb. 1863. This is a revised version, dated 1871.

    15. *bugle*: horn-shaped.
    17. *berg of hyaline*: iceberg of crystal.
    26. *beryl*: pale sea-green (from the stone).
    27. *Pactolus*: the golden river which healed Midas.

PAGE 38. HEAVEN-HAVEN. Oxford, July 1864. Early draft in Hopkins's first Oxford Diary, entitled 'Rest'. This slightly revised version belongs probably to 1865.

PAGE 39. 'WHERE ART THOU FRIEND . . . ?' Oxford, 24–27 April 1865. From Hopkins's second Oxford Diary; probably addressed to Digby Mackworth Dolben (see p. 3n.), whom Hopkins had met two months before. They did not meet again, but were intensely interested in each other's poetry and conversion to Catholicism. As Humphry House first pointed out, the sonnet follows closely on Hopkins's religious crisis of March 1865.

PAGE 39. THE ALCHEMIST IN THE CITY. Oxford, 15 May 1865. From the second Oxford Diary. The symbolism throws some light on Hopkins's later conflicts.

    39. *trees of Cerebinth*: turpentine trees.

PAGE 41. 'LET ME BE TO THEE AS THE CIRCLING BIRD.' Oxford, October–November 1865. From the second Oxford Diary. This sonnet shows the affinity of Hopkins's mind with George Herbert's: cf. Herbert's *Jordan* (1) and (2).

PAGE 41. THE HABIT OF PERFECTION. Oxford, January 1866.
    2. *whorlèd*: curved, curled.
    6. *shut* (noun): the act of closing, silencing.
    9. *shellèd*: encased.
    11. *ruck and reel*: whirling multitude of things.
    12. *Coils, keeps, and teases*: confuses, seizes hold of and distracts.
    13. *hutch*: store-house.

18. *stir and keep*: excitement and upkeep.

24. *And you . . .*: and you, hands, shall offer the sacraments at the Mass (*unhouse . . . the Lord*: take the consecrated Host from the tabernacle).

27-28. and provide the body, wedded to you, with clothes like the lilies of the fields, which shall be neither laboured at nor spun. Cf. Matt. vi. 28-29.

PAGE 43. THE WRECK OF THE DEUTSCHLAND. St. Beuno's College, North Wales, December-January, 1875-6. For Hopkins's account of his writing of the poem and of the 'Sprung Rhythm' in which it is composed, see letter to Dixon (pp. 158-9). Full reports of the wreck appeared in *The Times*, 8-13 December 1875: Hopkins had clearly read these or a similar account. The poem is at the same time clearly autobiographical: see his letter to Bridges, 21 August 1877 (p. 156). Hopkins's own spiritual crisis and conversion (Part the First) are, then, as important to it as the shipwreck itself (Part the Second), and both are given meaning as symbols of Christ's suffering. The 'tall nun's' indomitable faith and her vision of Christ's presence in the storm (st. 28) show that suffering experienced aright (st. 29)—as a re-enactment of Christ's Passion—is ultimately redemptive.

16. *laced*: drawn tight.

17. *his*: God's.

18. *hurtle*: clash.

20. *that spell*: during that time of anguish. Another interpretation has been put forward, making *spell* a verb = 'ascend' or 'mount', from 'speel' (Northern dialect, found in N. Wales).

23. *carrier-witted*: given the instinct of the carrier-pigeon.

24. *To flash . . . grace*: to fly from the flame of terror to the sacrificial fire of God, to rise from the grace of His wrath to the grace of His love.

25. *sift*: sand.

27. *mined*: undermined.

28. *combs*: rolls over (as a wave).

29. *I steady . . . pane*: Yet I am as steady as still water in a well, poised and balanced like a pane of glass.

30. *But roped with*: but connected with, fed by.

31. *Fells or flanks of the voel*: hillsides or mountain-sides. The Voel (Welsh: 'bare hill)' is a hill near St. Beuno's College.

31. *vein* (archaic): streamlet.

32. *gospel proffer*: the Gospel's offer, i.e. grace.

35. *wafting him*: taking in an intuition of God's presence.

39. *be instressed, stressed*: be impressed upon our being, 'come to stress' in us, through revelation.

42. *the stress felt*: the sudden revelation of God's presence.

47. *it rides time* . . .: it is beyond time, yet it controls time.

54–55. *Thence the discharge . . . flood yet*: Though the sudden presence of God had been felt before and is still powerfully felt, it burst into the world fully only through Christ's Incarnation and Passion.

56. *hard at bay*: tormented.

58–59. *We lash . . . last*: When we want to hurt someone, we keep back the word that stabs to the last.

59. *plush-capped*: with a velvety touch.

67. *dogged in den*: determined in sin.

73. *anvil-ding*: ringing stroke on anvil.

77–78. *Whether at once . . . skill*: whether his conversion is sudden, as was St. Paul's, or gradual and gentle, as was St. Augustine's.

79–80. *Make mercy . . . Mastery*: have mercy upon us all, master us all.

82. *The flange and the rail*: railway disaster.

88. *cringe*: probably 'make us cower' (obsolete).

93. *under thy feathers*: sheltered, under Thy wings.

95. *bay*: Church bay.

96. *rounds*: circles.

96. *reeve* (nautical metaphor): rope together.

101. *flint-flake*: flecked like grey stone.

106. *combs*: crests, ridges. Note the 'linked rhyme': 'leeward/ drew her D—': other examples are in stanzas 31 and 35. W. H. Gardner shows that Hopkins probably took this device from 19th century Welsh poetry (*G. M. Hopkins*, II, pp. 153–4).

107. *Kentish Knock*: sandbank in the Thames estuary.

111. *whorl*: propeller.

112. *wind*: steer.

127. *cobbled*: formed like, having the look of, pebbles.

128. *burl*: vortex.

128. *buck*: toss.

141. *after*: bent upon, pursuing.

143. *Never-eldering . . . youth*: describing the eternally young quality of the joy that the experience of the nun gives him, mixed with his grief.

145. 'Five German nuns . . . clasped hands and were drowned together, the chief sister, a gaunt woman 6 ft. high, calling out loudly and often "O Christ, come quickly!" till the end came' (*The Times*, 11 December 1875).

147. *hawling* (=hauling): dragging (her) out.

148. *sloggering*: buffeting.

150. *fetch* (archaic): device.

154. *coifèd*: with close-fitting cap.

155. Since exiled from Protestant Germany, they make the *Deutschland* a name doubly of despair.

157. Gertrude, the thirteenth-century Catholic saint, had lived in a convent near Eisleben, Luther's birthplace: for Hopkins, they are symbols of good and evil springing from the same source, like Cain and Abel.

165. *Orion*: the mythological Hunter (cf. the constellation named after him).

166. *Thy unchancelling . . . worth*: You drove the nuns out of their sanctuary (chancel), to test their devotion.

168. *scroll-leaved flowers, lily showers*: symbols of martyrdom.

169–70. i.e. 'Five! the very number of Christ's wounds'.

169. *finding*: the emblem by which we find Christ.

169. *sake*: outward sign (see note to *Henry Purcell*, p. 187).

171–2. Man gave the wounds, but Christ received them as a sacrifice.

173–6. The reference here, and in the next stanza, is to St. Francis (whose nuns these were) receiving the five stigmata as Christ's chosen one.

174. *Before-time-taken*: St. Francis died aged 44, after a life of supreme deprivation.

175. *cinquefoil*: fivefold.

176. *lamb's fleece . . . rose-flake*: both emblems of martyrdom.

179–80. *his Lovescape*: Christ's perfect love.

182. *And five-livèd . . .*: who in their five lives and martyrs' deaths are your cherished pride.

186. *forehead*: St. Beuno's stands on a hill.

192. *The cross to her . . .*: holding her crucifix to her, she calls on Christ to come, identifying the terror of her plight with His name and suffering.

194. *arch and original Breath*: Holy Spirit.

195. *of the being . . .*: of accepting death as her lover Christ had done.

196. *body of lovely Death*: Christ the crucified.

198. *we are perishing*: see Matt. viii. 25.

201–4. To imagine the vision of Heaven the nun might have had, think of the joy when the lowering ground-locked grey sky suddenly opens to reveal the dazzling blue sky of May, with all May's fresh and varied life.

207–8. Whatever you can conceive of as the heaven you desire, the treasure beyond human eye and ear.

208. *The treasure . . .*: see 1 Cor. ii. 9.

209–13. No, it was not such visions that inspired the nun's cry. It was not the momentary horror of danger that made her ask for ease: but her life of constant self-sacrifice, with all its jarring disappointments, the toll that time takes, leaving the heart dulled with sorrow.

213–14. *Then further . . .*: moreover, in such a life it is Christ's Passion that has the tenderer appeal in agonized, solitary prayer like this.

216. *burly*: tumult.

217–24. The broken phrases suggest the inexpressible miracle that the nun's vision is of Christ Himself, present in the storm.

226. *single eye*: Cf. Luke xi. 34: 'When the eye is single, thy whole body is full of light.'

227. *Read the unshapeable* . . .: She understood that terrible night, incomprehensible otherwise.

228. i.e. that it was Christ's will.

229–30. *Wording it* . . .: calling on Christ, the Word, who created present and past, heaven and earth, to express Himself.

231–2. *to the blast/ Tarpeïan-fast*: bound to the storm as if to the Tarpeian rock (from which traitors were thrown in ancient Rome).

237. The Feast of the Immaculate Conception, 8 December.

238–40. The nun, by uttering the cry kept within her has, as it were, given Christ a new birth.

245–7. The nun's cry, an echo of the tender, felicitous finger of Providence, has rung out like a bell to startle the lost sheep back to the fold.

250. *Yore-flood*: the Flood.

251. *The recurb* . . .: the ebb and flow of the tides.

253. *Stanching, quenching* . . .: steadying and controlling the ocean of man's restless mind.

256. *bodes but abides*: forebodes, knows the future, but bides His time.

259–60. *for the lingerer* . . .: for those who cannot make up their mind to accept Him, God comes with a love that goes beyond death and the dark.

261. *vein*: streamlet, spring (as in st. 4).

264. *fetched*: reached (used of waves). Its subject is Christ, the 'giant', its object the relative pronoun omitted after *mark*. The reference, as Philip M. Martin shows in *Mastery and Mercy*, 1957, p. 68, is to the risen Christ's preaching 'unto the spirits in prison' (1 Pet. iii. 9).

266. *Double-natured Name*: name of Christ, both God and man.

367. *heart-fleshed*: incarnate.

269. *Mid-numbered He* . . .: second Person of the Trinity.

272. *shire*: countryside.

276. *Our King* . . .: pray that Christ, our King, may return.

277. *cresseted*: lit, shining like a beacon.

PAGE 56. THE SILVER JUBILEE. St. Beuno's, N. Wales; published with a sermon given by Fr. John Morris, S.J. Hopkins also addressed poems in Welsh and Latin to the Bishop.

7. *Sprang*: The Roman Catholic hierarchy in England was restored in 1850.

18. *Wales*: The diocese of Shrewsbury included the six counties of

N. Wales. Hopkins complains that they are backward in restoring the old religion.

PAGE 57. PENMAEN POOL. Barmouth, N. Wales, August 1876.

9–12. The two mountains, Dyphwys and Cader Idris, face each other across Penmaen Pool.

17. *Charles's Wain*: the constellation known also as the Plough.

PAGE 58. GOD'S GRANDEUR. St. Beuno's, 23 February 1877.

2. *shook foil*: 'I mean foil in its sense of leaf or tinsel. . . . Shaken gold-foil gives off broad glares like sheet lightning and also, and this is true of nothing else, owing to its zigzag dints and creasings and net-work of small many cornered facets, a sort of fork lightning too' (letter to Bridges, 4 January 1883).

PAGE 59. THE STARLIGHT NIGHT. St. Beuno's, 24 February 1877.

4. *delves* (obsolete): mines.

6. Both the whitebeam and the abele (white poplar) have white silky hairs on the under-side of their leaves.

9. *What*? i.e. What must I offer?

11. *sallows*: willow-shoots.

12–13. Cf. Matt. xiii. 30.

13. *shocks*: sheaves of corn.

13. *paling*: fencing. Cf. the stanza in Hopkins's Oxford Diary, beginning 'The stars were packed so close that night' (p. 114).

PAGE 60. SPRING. N. Wales, May 1877.

PAGE 60. IN THE VALLEY OF THE ELWY. N. Wales, 23 May, 1877. 'The kind people of the sonnet were the Watsons of Shooter's Hill, London, nothing to do with the Elwy. The facts were as stated. You misunderstood the thought, which is very far fetched, i.e. the frame of the sonnet is a rule of three sum *wrong*, thus: As the sweet smell to those kind people so the Welsh landscape is NOT to the Welsh; and then the author and principle of all four terms is asked to bring the sum right' (postcard to Bridges, 8 April 1879).

PAGE 61. THE SEA AND THE SKYLARK. Rhyl, May 1877.

6–7. *His rash-fresh* . . .: excitedly play out the notes of his headlong new song as a newly rewound skein of silk unwinds in spiral folds from a reel. This is based upon the explanation Hopkins gave Bridges, in a letter of 27 November 1882, of the image as it appeared in his first, rejected version: 'the "new-skeinèd score" is the lark's song "which from his height gives the impression (not to me only) of something falling to the earth and not vertically quite but tricklingly or wavingly, something as a skein of silk ribbed by having been tightly wound on a narrow card or a notched holder or as twine or fishing tackle unwinding from a *reel* or *winch* or as pearls strung on a horsehair: the laps or folds are the notes or short measures and bars of them. The same is called a *score* in the musical sense of score and this score is "writ upon a liquid sky trembling to welcome it", only not horizontally.'

PAGE 62. THE WINDHOVER. St. Beuno's, May 1877. Described by Hopkins to Bridges in June 1879 as 'the best thing I ever wrote'. Most critics have agreed—despite their very different readings of the poem. Some of these are given in the Introduction, pp. 22–23; the most opposed of them spring from two contrasted interpretations of ll. 9–11 given below.

3. *Of the rolling . . .*: upon the steady air as it rolled level beneath him.

4. *how he rung . . .*: how he circled, hovering upon his rippling wing. 'Ring' (from falconry) is to rise in spirals; 'ring on the rein' (from the riding-school) is used of a horse circling at the end of a long rein.

6. *bow–bend*: bow-shaped bend.

9–11. The crux is the tense and meaning of *buckle*. (1) Many read it as indicative and give it its commonest meaning of 'collapse, give way under stress'. The lines, applying directly to the kestrel (obliquely to Hopkins himself), then seem to mean (paraphrased): 'The natural beauty and grace of your plumage crumple and bend as you swoop down; and the light that flashes from you then is a billion times lovelier and more daring than before, my cavalier.'

But (2) *buckle* may equally well be imperative and have one of its older meanings, (*a*) 'fasten, buckle on' (*trans.*), or (*b*) 'grapple, prepare for action' (*intrans.*). The lines then apply directly to Hopkins's own heart ('my heart in hiding'), now imagined as itself having the kestrel's qualities. This reading is supported by the metrical stresses falling on *here* ('in my heart'), *thee* and *my*. The meaning will be: (*a*) 'Buckle on, fasten to my heart the beauty and grace, pride and plumage, of the kestrel!' (the request being made to Christ) . . .; or (*b*) 'Oh, beauty and grace, pride and plumage of the kestrel, come to my heart and prepare for action there! And the light that will flash from you [my heart] then will be a billion times lovelier and more daring, my heart become cavalier.'

12–14. Whichever interpretation of ll. 9–11 we adopt—(2) (*a*), the active, personal request to Christ, seems to me the most characteristic of Hopkins—these two images enforce the point that the heart prepared for service and sacrifice shines brightest: 'No wonder: since sheer plodding toil makes the ploughshare gleam down the furrow (*sillion*);

and the cold-blue embers of a dying fire, as they fall, break apart, and blaze out golden and orange-red.'

13. *ah my dear*: either Christ, to whom the poem is addressed (cf. George Herbert, *Love* (2): 'Ah, my dear,/ I cannot look on Thee,); or his own heart, become cavalier (*O my chevalier!*) through Christ's having answered his request.

PAGE 63. PIED BEAUTY. St. Beuno's, Summer 1877.

2. *brinded* (archaic): brindled, streaked.

4. Cf. 'Chestnuts as bright as coals or spots of vermilion' (Journal, 17 September 1868).

PAGE 63. HURRAHING IN HARVEST. Vale of Clywd, 1 September 1877. 'The Hurrahing Sonnet was the outcome of half an hour of extreme enthusiam as I walked home alone one day from fishing in the Elwy' (letter to Bridges, 16 July 1878). For Hopkins's explanation of the 'outriding' feet he marked in the MSS. of this sonnet, see pp. 154-5.

PAGE 64. THE CAGED SKYLARK. St. Beuno's, 1877.

2. *bone-house*: body.

5. *turf*: the turf of grass traditionally placed in a lark's cage.

7. *deadly*: death-like.

PAGE 65. THE LANTERN OUT OF DOORS. St. Bueno's, ? Autumn 1877. Hopkins called it 'companion' to *The Candle Indoors*.

4. *wading*: moving (from Old English *wadan*, to walk).

9-12. *wind . . . after*: follow them as far as I can with my eyes. The verb is 'wind (my) eye after': and Hopkins defended its oddity (or 'distinctiveness') in a letter to Bridges of 15 February 1879: 'I mean that the eye winds/ only in the sense that its focus or point of sight winds and that coincides with a point of the object and winds with that. For the object, a lantern passing further and further away and bearing now east now west of one right line, is truly and properly described as winding.'

13. *Kind*: no doubt an intended pun, 'loving' or 'kin'.

PAGE 65. THE LOSS OF THE EURYDICE. Mount St. Mary's College, Derbyshire, April 1878. Many details of the wreck are taken from newspaper reports which appeared in, e.g., *The Times*, 25-27 March. 'To do the Eurydice any kind of justice you must not slovenly read it with the eyes but with your ears, as if the paper were declaiming it at you', Hopkins wrote to Bridges, 21 May 1878. (p. 158). Part of a note he added to his manuscript reads: 'The scanning runs on without break to the end of the stanza, so that each stanza is rather one long line rhymed in passage than four lines with rhymes at the end.'

6. *furled*: 'How are hearts of oak furled? Well, in sand and sea water. The image comes out true under the circumstances, otherwise it could not hold together. You are to suppose a stroke or blast in a forest of "hearts of oak" . . . which at one blow both lays them low and buries them in broken earth. *Furling* (*ferrule* is a blunder for *furl*, I think) is *proper* when said of sticks and staves' (to Bridges, 30 May 1878).

7–8. *And flock-bells . . .*: And sheep-bells from the seaward slopes of the high downs. . . .

12. *lade* (archaic): load.

25. *bald—*: streaked with white.

27–28. *Hailropes . . . grind . . .*: cf. Hopkins's Oxford Diary entry: '*Grando* [Latin: hail] meaning splinters, fragments, little pieces detached in grinding, hence applied to hail.'

29–32. *Carisbrook . . . Boniface Down*: all places in the Isle of Wight. The *Eurydice* went down off Dunnose, near Ventnor.

34. *royals*: royal sails.

40. *messes*: i.e. the ship's messes.

47. *Cheer's death*: despair.

48. *champ-white*: churned to a white foam (from 'to champ', to chew—dialect).

50–51. *Right, rude of feature . . .*: He thought he heard Duty, stern of face, say . . .

53–56. Of this stanza Hopkins wrote to Bridges, 30 May 1878: 'You mistake the sense of this as I feared it would be mistaken. I believed Hare to be a brave and conscientious man: what I say is that *even* those who seem unconscientious will act the right part at a great push.'

68. *rivelling* (archaic): causing his eyes (or skin) to wrinkle.

79. *dawning*: the morning.

85–88. The disaster to the *Eurydice*—so many young men drowned without absolution—underlines for Hopkins the national disaster: that England has abandoned the Roman Catholic religion.

89–92. *bygones . . .*: the Reformation and its consequences—the neglect or, worse, appropriation of ancient and hallowed Catholic churches.

99–100. *riving off . . .*: the tearing away (from Catholicism) of a people who were once so responsive to Christ's truth and grace.

101. *starlight-wender*: traveller by starlight.

102. *The marvellous Milk . . .*: 'in Catholic times Walsingham Way was a name for the Milky Way, as being supposed a finger-post to our Lady's shrine at Walsingham [Norfolk]' (letter to Bridges, 30 May 1878).

NHS

103. *one*: Duns Scotus. See *Duns Scotus's Oxford*, l. 14.

105. *O well wept,* . . .: You do well to weep, mother who has lost a son (relative pronoun omitted as in next).

112. *O Hero savest*: O Hero that savest.

114–15. *Have . . . heard*: may you have heard (for the grammar, see Hopkins's explanation of 'Have fair fallen' in *Henry Purcell*, p. 74).

117–20. Not that those in hell can be redeemed; but prayer, renewed till the day of Last Judgement, will bring eternal pity for souls sunk in delusion (i.e. who have not found Catholic truth).

PAGE 70. THE MAY MAGNIFICAT. Stonyhurst, May 1878. Written to be hung up before the statue of the Virgin Mary at Stonyhurst in May. Hopkins described it to Bridges, 29 January 1879, as 'a May piece . . . in which I see little good but the freedom of the rhythm'.

21. *bugle*: a plant which bears thick blue spikes in May.

39. *thorp*: hamlet.

40. *surfèd*: i.e. with blossom-like foam.

41. *greybell*: the bud of the bluebell as it opens.

PAGE 72. BINSEY POPLARS. Oxford, March 1879.

6. *sandalled*: woven in strips, as webbing on sandals; dappled.

14–15. *That, like this sleek* . . .: That, just as a mere prick will take away all power of sight from this smooth eyeball, . . .

21. *únselve*: destroy the self hood of.

22. *especial*: individual (the attribute of an object which gives it what Duns Scotus called *haecceitas*, 'thisness'). The destruction of the poplars destroys what gives the scene its true meaning.

PAGE 73. DUNS SCOTUS'S OXFORD. Oxford, March 1879. Johannes Duns Scotus (?1275–?1308), Scholastic philosopher, nicknamed 'the Subtle Doctor'; said to have been a Fellow of Merton College, Oxford, and in 1301 University Professor of Divinity. He wrote works on logic and metaphysics, and two commentaries on the *Sentences* of Peter Lombard. Hopkins first read the latter in August 1872, and 'was flush with a new stroke of enthusiasm' (see his Journal entry, p. 135). For the immensely important influence of Scotus's thought on his poetry, see Introduction, pp. 8 and 25, and Christopher Devlin, S.J., *Sermons and Devotional Writings*, passim.

3–4. *that country and town* . . .: in which country and town once met and set off and balanced their characteristics in equal measure.

6. *neighbour-nature*: nature of good neighbourliness (between country and town).

8. *keeping* (archaic): dwelling. Hopkins uses the same word, in the sense

of a quality of *belonging*, of the epithets and images in William Barnes's
Dorset poems (letter to Coventry Patmore, 6 October 1886, p. 166).

12. *realty*: reality.

14. Duns Scotus was the champion of the Immaculate Conception.

PAGE 74. HENRY PURCELL. Oxford, April 1879. 'The sonnet on
Purcell means this: 1–4. I hope Purcell is not damned for being a
Protestant, because I love his genius. 5–8. And that not so much for
gifts he shares, even though it should be in higher measure, with other
musicians as for his own individuality. 9–14. So that while he is aiming
only at impressing me his hearer with the meaning in hand I am looking
out meanwhile for his specific, his individual markings and mottlings,
"the sakes of him". It is as when a bird thinking only of soaring spreads
its wings: a beholder may happen then to have his attention drawn
by the act to the plumage displayed' (letter to Bridges, 4 January 1883).

1. *Have fair fallen*: May fair fortune have befallen. For the same
unusual grammar, explained by Hopkins in another letter to Bridges
see the penultimate stanza of *The Loss of the Eurydice*.

2. *arch-especial*: see *Binsey Poplars*, note on l. 22.

3. *with the reversal . . .*: (May Purcell have died a good death), so that
the heavy condemnation under which he outwardly or nominally lay
for being out of the true Church may in consequence of his good
intentions have been reversed.

4. *low lays him*: which lays him low.

4. *listed*: enlisted.

6. *nursle*: cherish.

9–14. 'The sestet . . . is not so clearly worked out as I could wish.
The thought is that as the seabird opening his wings with a whiff
of wind in your face means the whirr of the motion, but also unaware
gives you a whiff of knowledge about his plumage, the marking of
which stamps his species, that he does not mean, so Purcell, seemingly
intent only on the thought or feeling he is to express or call out, incidentally lets you remark the individualizing marks of his own genius'
(letter to Bridges, 26 May 1879; the quotations below are from the
same letter).

10. *sakes*: 'It is the *sake* of "for the sake of", *forsake, namesake, keepsake*.
I mean by it the being a thing has outside itself, as a voice by its echo,
a face by its reflection, a body by its shadow, a man by his name, fame,
or memory, *and also* that in the thing by virtue of which especially
it has this being abroad, and that is something distinctive, marked,
specifically or individually speaking, as for a voice and echo clearness;
for a reflected image light, brightness; for a shadow-casting body bulk;
for a man of genius, great achievements, amiability, and so on. In this
case it is, as the sonnet says, distinctive quality in genius.'

10. *moonmarks*: 'I mean crescent shaped marking on the quill-feathers, either in the colouring of the feather or made by the overlapping of one on another.'

13. *wuthering*: 'a Northcountry word for the noise and rush of wind.'

PAGE 75. THE CANDLE INDOORS. Oxford, 1879: sent to Bridges (with *The Handsome Heart*) in letter of 22 June. Hopkins described it to him as 'a companion' to *The Lantern out of Doors*.

4. *to-fro tender trambeams* . . .: delicate silk-like beams of light from the candle flicker to and fro at the least motion of the eyelids (*tram* probably in its sense of fine silk threads loosely twisted together; *truckle at*: timidly draw back from).

8. / : this oblique stroke, often used by Hopkins in his Journal, indicates a brief pause.

8. *aggrandise*: magnify.

9. *Come you indoors*: look into your own heart first! (addressing himself).

9–14. Cf. the Sermon on the Mount: Matt. v. 13–16 and vii. 1–5.

13. *deft-handed:* quick to react.

PAGE 75. THE HANDSOME HEART. Oxford, 1879. 'Last Lent . . . two boys of our congregation gave me much help in the sacristy in Holy Week. I offered them money for their services, which the elder refused, but being pressed consented to take it laid out in a book. The younger followed suit; then when some days after I asked him what I should buy answered as in the sonnet' (letter to Bridges, 14 August 1879).

5. *carriers*: carrier-pigeons. Cf. *carrier-witted* in *The Wreck of the Deutschland*, st. 3.

6. *Doff darkness*: throw off sin.

7. *self-instressed*: impelled by its own natural impulse.

8. *Falls light* . . .: acts gracefully.

12–13. *or gain/ Not granted*!: or gift which will not be granted!

14. *strain*: natural quality.

PAGE 76. THE BUGLER'S FIRST COMMUNION. Oxford, 27 July 1879.

1. *barrack*: Cowley Barracks, Hopkins told Bridges. He was working as a priest at St. Aloysius's Church, Oxford.

12. *housel* (archaic): the consecrated wafer of the Eucharist.

13. *sendings*: i.e. of grace.

18. *squander*: scatter.

18. *sally*: that sally (relative pronoun omitted).

19. *limber*: pliant, responsive.

29–30. *strains Us*: exerts us to respond.

30. *fretted in a bloomfall*: in all the variety of its flushed beauty.

37. *least . . . lift*: least quickenings lift me.

42. *rankle*: become bitter.

43. *in backwheels*: backwards.

44. *That left . . .*: Leaving that . . ., I can rest here.

46. *brandle* (obsolete): shake.

46. *with ride and jar*: with the force of their shock.

48. *Forward-like . . .*: Perhaps I have been over-eager, but that is how I feel; and most likely Heaven was favourable and heard my prayers.

PAGE 78. MORNING, MIDDAY, AND EVENING SACRIFICE. Oxford, August 1879. Each stanza commands the giving of its subject's appropriate gifts to God: st. 1, the beauty of youth; st. 2, the power of the prime of life; st. 3, the matured mind.

2. *wimpled*: curved.

6. *fuming*: passing away like smoke.

17. *silk-ash*: 'I meant to compare grey hairs to the flakes of silky ash which may be seen round wood embers burnt in a clear fire' (letter to Bridges, 22 October 1879): i.e. under grey hairs the mind preserves its heat, and, under its tough, outer covering, its maturity.

21. *Your offering . . .*: 'is said like "Your ticket", "Your reasons", "Your money or your life" . . .: it is "Come, your offer of all this (the matured mind), and without delay either!"' (ibid.).

PAGE 79. ANDROMEDA. Oxford, 12 August 1879. 'I enclose a sonnet on which I invite minute criticism. I endeavoured in it a more Miltonic plainness and severity than I have anywhere else. I cannot say it has turned out severe, still less plain, but it seems almost free from quaintness and in aiming at one excellence I may have hit another' (letter to Bridges, 14 August 1879). Andromeda, the beautiful daughter of Cepheus, King of Ethiopia, was chained to a rock by her father to appease a sea-monster sent by Poseidon to ravage the country. She was rescued by Perseus, who slew the monster and married her. In Hopkins's sonnet *Time's Andromeda* is the Catholic Church; *this rock rude*, St. Peter, on whom it was founded; *a wilder beast from West*, the new enemies of the Church—rationalism and materialism; and Perseus, Christ.

10. Perseus possessed winged sandals.

13–14. *then to alight . . .*: Then he will descend suddenly, and, with the weapons with which he slew the Gorgon, will sever Andromeda's bonds and render harmless the monster's fangs: i.e. Christ at His second coming will redeem His Church and destroy her enemies.

14. *barebill*: the sword or sickle with which Perseus had cut off the Gorgon Medusa's head. Hopkins's oblique mark makes clear that

thongs and fangs are not in apposition to *gear and barebill*, but the object of *disarming*.

PAGE 80. PEACE. Oxford, 1879.

2. *under be*: be under.

4. *own my heart*: my own heart. *Under* and *own* are both transposed for the sake of the rhythm.

7. *reaving*: robbing me of.

8. *plumes*: dresses its feathers as a welcome.

PAGE 80. AT THE WEDDING MARCH. Bedford Leigh, Lancashire, 21 October 1879.

PAGE 81. FELIX RANDAL. Liverpool, April 1880.

1. *farrier*: blacksmith.

3. *reason rambled in it*:: his mind began to ramble.

6. *and all*: Lancashire dialect—as is *all road ever* (l. 8): in whatever way.

7. *our sweet reprieve and ransom*: Holy Communion and the gifts it brings.

9. *us too it endears*: it adds to our own worth.

13. *random*: probably heedless, thoughtless (taking up Felix Randal's lack of forethought of the previous line), rather than architecturally irregular (which it could also mean).

14. *fettle*: prepare.

PAGE 82. BROTHERS. Hampstead, August 1880. Hopkins wrote the first draft of this poem in August 1879 in stanzas 'in Wordsworth's manner'. He described it to Bridges as 'a little scene that touched me at Mount St. Mary's [Derbyshire]'. (14 August 1879).

6. *Our boys' plays*: at Mount St. Mary's College, Chesterfield, where Hopkins was 'sub-minister' during part of 1878.

38. *framed in fault*: fallen (through original sin).

PAGE 83. SPRING AND FALL. Lydiate, Lancashire, September 1880.

8. *wanwood* (noun) seems to fuse together the meanings of *wan* as an adjective—dismal, faded, dark—and the obsolete prefix *wan-*, expressing negation or deficiency: perhaps the faded, rotting leaves of trees that have lost their foliage.

8. *leafmeal* (adverb): leaf by leaf (cf. piecemeal).

11. *are the same*: i.e. are *all* the same.

12–13. *Nor mouth had, . . .*: No one had said nor had even the mind grasped what the heart and spirit knew or guessed by instinct.

13. *ghost* (archaic): the (living) spirit.

PAGE 84. INVERSNAID. 28 September 1881. Inversnaid is a hamlet in Stirlingshire on the east side of Loch Lomond. The brief visit which inspired this poem was made from Glasgow in the late summer of 1881. Much later (7 September 1887) Hopkins wrote to A. W. M. Baillie: 'The day was dark and partly hid the lake, yet it did not altogether disfigure it but gave a pensive or solemn beauty which left a deep impression on me.'

2. *rollrock*: rolling rocks out of its channel.

3. *coop*: hollow, enclosed space.

3. *comb*: crest.

4. *flutes*: forms grooves or channels.

6. *twindles*: a compound of 'twists' and 'dwindles'; or, possibly, forms twin parts (from the archaic noun *twindle*, a twin).

9. *degged* (Lancashire dialect): sprinkled.

11. *heathpacks*: clumps of heather.

11. *flitches*: strips, patches.

12. *beadbonny ash*: the mountain ash, beautiful with bead-like berries.

PAGE 85. 'AS KINGFISHERS CATCH FIRE.' No title or date. This sonnet—essential to an understanding of Hopkins—is the clearest statement of the theological support he found in Duns Scotus for his own poetical beliefs: all created things exist to express their own natures; and man's expression of his nature finds its highest perfection in the Incarnation of Christ. The poem's imagery is strikingly similar to a passage on 'Contemplation for Obtaining Love' from Hopkins's commentary on the *Spiritual Exercises*: 'All things therefore are charged with love, are charged with God and if we know how to touch them give off sparks and take fire, yield drops and flow, ring and tell of him' (the passage before this is dated 8 December 1881).

3. *tucked* (dialect): plucked.

3. *tells*: sounds out.

6. *each one*: where (omitted).

7. *selves*: expresses its own nature.

9. *justices*: used here in a special theological sense: 'to act in a godly manner, live fully energized by grace, justness, sanctity' (R. V. Schoder, S.J., in *Immortal Diamond*).

12–14. Through the Incarnation Christ expresses the perfect beauty which all men may attain.

PAGE 86. RIBBLESDALE. Stonyhurst, 1882. Ribblesdale is the Lancashire dale in which Stonyhurst College lies: Hopkins taught there 1882–4. In two MSS. of the poem he quotes, in Latin, Rom. viii. 19 and 20: 'For the earnest expectation of the creation waiteth for the revealing of the Sons of God, For the creation was subjected to vanity, not of its own will, but by reason of him who subjected it.'

1. *throng* (adjective): dense (Lancashire dialect).

2. *louchèd*: 'a coinage of mine and is to mean much the same as *slouched, slouching*' (letter to R. W. Dixon, 25 June 1883). As Bridges noted, it is used in dialect.

6–8. *with him who . . .*: with God who shaped—still shapes—your lovely dale to slope down like this and is responsible for this wild rush of your river, and can abandon, if He wishes, everything to wrack and ruin.

7. *down*: adverb, going with *dealt* in l. 6.

11. *selfbent*: self-will, self-interest.

11. *turn*: natural inclination.

12. *reave . . . bare*: strip bare, despoil.

13. *none reck of world after*: give no thought to eternity.

14. *Earth*: governs wear.

PAGE 86. THE LEADEN ECHO AND THE GOLDEN ECHO. Stonyhurst, 13 October 1882. 'St. Winefred's Well' was to be a verse drama; Hopkins wrote only fragments of it, between 1879 and 1885. Of this song he wrote to R. W. Dixon: 'I never did anything more musical'; and—in answer to Bridges's charge that in its irregular rhythms he had been influenced by Walt Whitman— 'That piece of mine is very highly wrought. The long lines are not rhythm run to seed: everything is weighed and timed in them. Wait till they have taken hold of your ear and you will find it so. No, but what it *is* like is the rhythm of Greek tragic choruses or of Pindar: which is pure sprung rhythm. And that has the same changes of cadence from point to point as this piece. If you want to try it, read one till you have settled the true places of the stress, mark these, then read it aloud, and you will see. Without this these choruses are prose bewitched; with it they are sprung rhythm like that piece of mine' (18 October 1882).

The Leaden Echo

'I cannot satisfy myself about the first line. You must know that words like *charm* and *enchantment* will not do: the thought is of beauty as of something that can be physically kept and lost and by physical things only, like keys; then the things must come from the *mundus muliebris*; and thirdly they must not be markedly oldfashioned. You will see that this limits the choice of words very much indeed. . . . *Back* is not pretty, but it gives that feeling of physical constraint which I want' (letter to Bridges, 26 November 1882). This remark tells us a great deal about Hopkins's use of language.

1. *brace*: clasp, buckle.

3–4. *frowning . . . Down*: rebuke.

12. *ruck*: crease, fold.

The Golden Echo

1. *Spare!*: stop despairing!

8. *seems to us*: 'that' omitted; the relative clause continues until the main verb, *fleets*, l. 12, governed by *everything*.

10. *wimpled-water-dimpled*: both 'wimple' and 'dimple' are used of streams forming ripples.

11. *fleet* (archaic): glide away.

13. *its own best being*: i.e. the body after the Resurrection.

18. *beauty-in-the-ghost*: spiritual beauty (ghost: the living spirit, as in *Spring and Fall*, l. 13).

22–23. *Nay, what we had . . .*: 'Nay more: the seed that we so carelessly and freely flung into the dull furrow, and then forgot it, will have come to ear meantime' (letter to Bridges, 21 October 1882).

23–25. *what . . . what*: i.e. the seed (*what we had . . . left* of l. 22).

26. *fashed* (dialect): troubled.

26. *cogged* (archaic): deceived.

27. *the thing we freely forfeit*: the beauty we give back to God without loss.

PAGE 88. THE BLESSED VIRGIN COMPARED TO THE AIR WE BREATHE. Stonyhurst, 1883. A 'Maypiece', written to be hung up in honour of the Virgin, as was *The May Magnificat* four years earlier.

5. *flixed*: from 'flix', fur—one of Hopkins's favourite words to describe clouds in his Journal (e.g. 'a high-blown crest of flix or fleece', September 1869).

7. *riddles*: pierces, perforates.

40–41. *Since God has let . . .*: Since God dispenses His providence in accordance with her prayers.

53–54. *Yet no part . . .*: Yet all the grace she gives is ultimately Christ's.

56. *fresh* (adverb): afresh.

79. *sapphire-shot*: woven (like shot silk) with threads of sapphire-blue.

100. *flecks*: probably in its dialect sense of flares, sudden bursts of flame (emitted from the burning coal).

101. *Quartz-fret*: interlaced pattern of quartz (*fret* is often used to describe clouds in the Journal).

108. *bare*: revealed directly.

PAGE 92. SPELT FROM SYBIL'S LEAVES. Dublin, Winter 1884–5. 'Of this long sonnet above all remember what applies to all my verse,

Oнs

that it is, as living art should be, made for performance and that its performance is not reading with the eye but loud, leisurely, poetical (not rhetorical) recitation, with long rests, long dwells on the rhyme and other marked syllables, and so on. This sonnet should be almost sung: it is most carefully timed in *tempo rubato* [irregular rhythm]' (letter to Bridges, 11 December 1886).

For an excellent short discussion of this fine poem—the first of the self-torturing sonnets written during Hopkins's last years in Dublin—see F. R. Leavis, *New Bearings in English Poetry*, pp. 182–6.

Title: probably a reference to the prophetic books of the Cumaean Sybil, who guided Aeneas to the underworld (Virgil, *Aeneid*, VI). W. H. Gardner points out also the relevance of the *Dies irae*: 'As David and the Sybil testify . . . what terror shall affright the soul when the judge comes.'

1. *attuneable*: harmonious, blended.

3. *Her fond yellow hornlight . . . west*: surely the soft light of the setting sun (he uses 'horns' of the sun's long curves of light in his Journal, 30 June 1866). F. R. Leavis (see above) and some other critics have interpreted it as the setting moon: but the whole phrase suggests the last rays of the dying sun.

3. *hoarlight*: cold, grey starlight.

6. *throughther* (Scots dialect): through each other. Earth's varied forms are all gone, merged into each other.

6. *páshed*: beaten.

7. *Disremembering* (Irish): forgetting.

7. *round* (archaic): whisper warningly.

9. *damask* (verb): pattern, as with damascene work on a blade.

10. *Our tale . . . !*: this is a parable, a prophecy, for our own situation.

11. *part, pen, pack . . .*: let life divide all it contains into two flocks.

13. *ware of*: guard against.

14. *sheathe—and shelterless*: sheathless and shelterless.

PAGE 93 . TO WHAT SERVES MORTAL BEAUTY ? 23 August 1885.

2. *the O-seal-that-so feature*: the features whose beauty makes the artist exclaim, 'O, seal them, perpetuate them, for ever'.

2–3. *flung prouder form . . .*: form that moves with a prouder grace even than one set dancing by Purcell's music.

4–5. *a glance . . .*: a single glance at such beauty may conquer us more completely than a long, disconcerting gaze (at the less beautiful).

7. *Gregory*: Gregory I (Pope, *c.* 590–604), who, on seeing the fair British slaves for sale in Rome, made his famous pun, '*Non Angli sed Angeli*', and sent Augustine as the first Christian missionary to Britain.

11. *men's selves. Self . . .*: cf. '*As kingfishers catch fire*', ll. 7–8.

12. *own*: accept (governing *gift*).

13–14. *then leave, . . .*: then let beauty alone. But not utterly: wish rather for it—as for all things—the higher beauty, God's grace.

PAGE 94. THE SOLDIER. Clongowes, Ireland, August 1885.
    6. *dears the artist . . .*: holds the artist dear for the sake of his art.
    8. *And scarlet wear . . .*: 'find' understood, from l. 7.
    10. *reeve* (nautical): pass (a rope) through a block.
    14. *this*: in the likeness of a soldier.

PAGE 95. CARRION COMFORT. ?1885. On 17 Mary 1885 Hopkins told Bridges: 'I have after long silence written two sonnets, which I am touching: if ever anything was written in blood one of these was.' Bridges suggested that this was the sonnet 'written in blood': but it seems equally likely—perhaps more likely—that Hopkins was referring to the next, even more desolate, sonnet, written on the same MS. page as a revised version of this.
    5. *O thou terrible*: God, with whom he is wrestling.
    5. *rude* (used as an adverb): violently.
    6. *wring-world*: world-wringing.

PAGE 96. 'NO WORST, THERE IS NONE.' ?1885. For Hopkins's possible description of this sonnet, see note to last.
    2. *schooled at forepangs*: taught by past pangs which looked forward to these.
    5. *herds-long*: following each other like cattle in a herd.
    8. *force*: of necessity.

PAGE 96. 'TO SEEM THE STRANGER.' ?1885. This and the three following sonnets were found together among Hopkins's papers after his death. They were probably among those he referred to in a letter to Bridges of 1 September 1885: 'Four of these came like inspirations unbidden and against my will. And in the life I lead now, which is one of a continually jaded and harassed mind, if in any leisure I try to do anything I make no way—nor with my work, alas! but so it must be.'
    3. *in Christ not near*: i.e. they were not Roman Catholics: his parents had been deeply distressed by his conversion.
    4. *he my peace/ my parting*: Christ who should have brought me peace has become the cause of my estrangement. The pause indicated by Hopkins's oblique stroke stresses the paradox.
    8. *wars*: i.e. the Irish struggle for Home Rule. Hopkins felt deeply the conflict between his sympathy for the Catholic Irish and his loyalty to England. Though bitterly opposed to Gladstone's policy, he saw Home Rule as the only alternative to bloodshed.

11–14. *Only what word/ Wisest* . . .: F. R. Leavis compares this to *Macbeth*, I. iii. 138–41 ('My thought, whose murder yet is but fantastical, . . .') in the 'rendering of the very movement of consciousness' (*New Bearings in English Poetry*, p. 170). As W. H. Gardner has suggested (*G. M. Hopkins*, II, 345), the frustration is of *all* Hopkins's creative talents: philosophical as well as poetic and musical.

14. *began*: whether a verb following an omitted relative pronoun, or a noun, the sense is 'one who only began'.

PAGE 97. 'I WAKE AND FEEL THE FELL OF DARK.' ?1885.

1. *fell*: animal hide (its meanings of 'fierce' and 'having fallen' are also present).

7. *dead*: undelivered.

12. *Selfyeast of spirit* . . .: i.e. the heavy, flat dough of my bodily self sours the spirit which should leaven it: 'a dull dough' is Hopkins's correction for his original 'my selfstuff'.

13. *The lost*: the damned, in Hell.

14. *but worse*: the agonies of the damned must be worse than his; but the pressure of the comparison Hopkins has built up all but eliminates the difference.

PAGE 97. 'PATIENCE, HARD THING!' ?1885.

2–3. *Patience who asks*: he who asks for patience.

8. *Purple eyes*: the ivy's small purple berries.

10. *dearer* (archaic): more grievously.

11. *even so*: i.e. whatever the cost in mortification.

12. *he*: i.e. God (compared here to a bee distilling honey from man's patience).

14. *combs*: honeycombs.

PAGE 98. 'MY OWN HEART LET ME MORE HAVE PITY ON.' ?1885.

6. *comfortless*: 'world' understood, to complete the parallel with *dark* in the next line.

7–8. *or thirst can find* . . .: a reminiscence of *The Ancient Mariner*: 'Water, water everywhere, | Nor any drop to drink.'

9. *Jackself*: common, humdrum self.

11. *Size*: grow.

12. *At God knows when* . . .: whenever and however God wills it.

13. *wrung*: forced.

13–14. *unforeseen times rather* . . .: unexpectedly, rather—as patches of sky seen between them dapple the mountains—joy's smile lights up a lovely mile around. (*betweenpie* is a verb coined by Hopkins from *between* and *pied*.)

PAGE 98. TOM'S GARLAND. Dromore, September 1887. Hopkins sent Bridges his own explanation of this difficult sonnet with two codas in a letter to him of 10 February 1888: 'I laughed outright and often, but very sardonically, to think you and the Canon could not construe my last sonnet; that he had to write to you for a crib. It is plain I must go no farther on this road: if you and he cannot understand me who will? Yet, declaimed, the strange constructions would be dramatic and effective. Must I interpret it? It means then that, as St. Paul and Plato and Hobbes and everybody says, the commonwealth or well ordered human society is like one man; a body with many members and each its function; some higher, some lower, but all honourable, from the honour which belongs to the whole. The head is the sovereign, who has no superior but God and from heaven receives his or her authority: we must then imagine this head as bare (see St. Paul much on this) and covered, so to say, only with the sun and stars, of which the crown is a symbol, which is an ornament but not a covering; it has an enormous hat or skull cap, the vault of heaven. The foot is the daylabourer, and this is armed with hobnail boots, because it has to wear and be worn by the ground; which again is symbolical; for it is navvies or daylabourers who, on the great scale or in gangs and millions, mainly trench, tunnel, blast, and in other ways disfigure, "mammock" the earth and, on a small scale, singly, and superficially stamp it with their footprints. And the "garlands" of nails they wear are therefore the visible badge of the place they fill, the lowest in the commonwealth. But this place still shares the common honour, and if it wants one advantage, glory or public fame, makes up for it by another, ease of mind, absence of care; and these things are symbolized by the gold and the iron garlands. (O, once explained, how clear it all is!) Therefore the scene of the poem is laid at evening, when they are giving over work and one after another pile their picks, with which they earn their living, and swing off home, knocking sparks out of mother earth not now by labour and of choice but by the mere footing, being strong-shod and making no hardship of hardness, taking all easy. And so to supper and bed. Here comes a violent but effective hyperbaton or suspension, in which the action of the mind mimics that of the labourer—surveys his lot, low but free from care; then by a sudden strong act throws it over the shoulder or tosses it away as a light matter. The witnessing of which lightheartedness makes me indignant with the fools of Radical Levellers. But presently I remember that this is all very well for those who are in, however low in, the Commonwealth and share in any way the common weal; but that the curse of our times is that many do not share it, that they are outcasts from it and have neither security nor splendour; that they share care with the high and insecurity with the low, but wealth or comfort with neither. And this state of things, I say, is the origin of Loafers, Tramps, Cornerboys, Roughs, Socialists and other pests of society. And I think that it is a very pregnant sonnet, and in point of execution very highly wrought, too much so, I am afraid.'

1. *steel*: i.e. his hobnail boots.

2. *fallowbootfellow*: his workfellow wearing similar clay-caked boots.

3. *rips out rockfire*: knocks sparks out of the rocky earth.

5–6. *feel/ That . . . hunger*: an adjectival phrase governing *Tom*.

8–9. *Commonweal/ Little I reck . . .*: I reckon that the country would be little lacking in its duty.

12. *mammocks*: treads, breaks up (governing *mother-ground*).

12–14. *But no way sped . . .*: But consider the fate of the unemployed. They have nothing to help them: neither the ruler's mind nor the worker's strength; neither the splendour and responsibility of high place, nor the security of an obscure and low one.

PAGE 99. HARRY PLOUGHMAN. Dromore, September 1887. Hopkins thought well of this sonnet. On 28 September 1887 he described it to Bridges as 'a direct picture of a ploughman, without afterthought'. On 11 October he wrote to him: 'The rhythm of this sonnet, which is altogether for recital, not for perusal (as by nature verse should be) is very highly studied. From much considering it I can no longer gather any impression of it: perhaps it will strike you as intolerably violent and artificial.' And on 6 November: 'I want Harry Ploughman to be a vivid figure before the mind's eye; if he is not that the sonnet fails.'

1. *flue*: down, fluff.

3. *knee-nave*: kneecap.

4. *Head and foot . . . shank*: the first of the 5 extra half-lines in this sonnet. Hopkins described them to Bridges as 'burden-lines', and said 'they might be recited by a chorus . . . There is in this very heavily loaded sprung rhythm a call for their employment.'

10. *features* (verb): mirrors, shows.

13. *quail*: submit, yield.

13. *'s cheek*: his cheek.

13–14. *curls . . . /crossbridle*: his curls tumble over his head or twist themselves.

15. *See his wind-lilylocks-laced*: see his locks, fair as lilies, laced by the wind. 'Dividing a compound word by a clause sandwiched into it was a desperate deed, I feel, and I do not feel that it was an unquestionable success', Hopkins wrote to Bridges, presumably referring to this line.

16. *Churlsgrace*: from 'churl' (archaic), peasant.

17. *Them—broad in bluff hide . . .*: his feet, lashed in boots of bluff hide with frowning creases.

17–19. *raced/ With, along them* . . .: as they race along with the ploughshare and the cold, wet, shining earth upturned by it in the furrow.

PAGE 100. THAT NATURE IS A HERACLITEAN FIRE AND OF THE COMFORT OF THE RESURRECTION. Co. Dublin, 26 July 1888. Sonnet with three codas.

Title: According to the Greek philosopher Heraclitus (*c.* 535–*c.* 475 B.C.) all nature, including the human body and soul, is ultimately resolvable into fire, the rational principle which governs the universe. All is therefore in a state of flux: fire continually changes into water, water into earth, and then the process is reversed. Nothing can escape final destruction.

1. *chevy*: race.

4. *Shivelights*: strips of light.

4. *shadowtackle*: shadow-patterns.

5. *ropes*: twists, churns up into rope-like shapes.

6. *rutpeel*: the flattened mud of ruts.

6. *parches*: (the wind) dries up.

7. *stanches, starches*: makes firm and stiff (*wind* is still the subject).

8. *squadroned masks*: the multitude of impressions.

8. *manmarks treadmire toil* . . .: relative pronoun probably omitted: the footmarks of man left by his toiling in the mud.

11. *his firedint*: the spark or fire given out by his being.

14. *disseveral* (coined word): separate and unique.

18. *Across my foundering deck*: cf. the shipwreck as symbol in *The Deutschland* and *The Eurydice*.

23. *Jack*: common man.

23. *patch* (archaic): fool.

PAGE 102. ST. ALPHONSUS RODRIGUEZ. Dublin, 1888. On 3 October 1888 Hopkins wrote to Bridges: 'I ask your opinion of a sonnet written to order on the occasion of the first feast since his canonisation proper of St. Alphonsus Rodriguez, a laybrother of our Order, who for 40 years acted as hall-porter to the College of Palma in Majorca: he was, it is believed, much favoured by God with heavenly light and much persecuted by evil spirits. The sonnet (I say it snorting) aims at being intelligible.'

1. *so we say*: 'I mean "This is what we commonly say, but we are wrong"'.

10. *trickling increment*: gradual growth.

PAGE 102. 'THOU ART INDEED JUST, LORD.' 17 March 1889. 'Observe, it must be read *adagio molto* and with great stress', Hopkins wrote to Bridges on 20 March 1889. The Latin quotation given at the head of the sonnet is from Jer. xiii. 1: 'Righteous art thou, O Lord, when I plead with thee: yet let me talk with thee of thy judgements: Wherefore doth the way of the wicked prosper? wherefore are all they happy that deal very treacherously?'

8. *spare*: idle.

11. *fretty chervil*: cow-parsley with fretted leaves.

13. *Time's eunuch*: on 1 September 1885 Hopkins had written to Bridges: 'if I could but get on, if I could but produce work I should not mind its being buried, silenced, and going no further; but it kills me to be time's eunuch and never to beget'.

PAGE 103. 'THE SHEPHERD'S BROW.' 3 April 1889. Not included among Hopkins's finished poems by Bridges, on the grounds that it 'must have been thrown off one day in a cynical mood, which he could not have wished permanently to intrude among his last serious poems'. But, as the last of five full drafts, it was hardly 'thrown off'; and, however cynical or despairing its mood, that seems no justification for continuing to exclude it from the canon.

6. *groundlong*: sprawling (the sound-association with 'groundling' clearly links it with *life's masque* in l. 13).

8. *What bass . . .*: What humdrum experience [compared with lightning or the fall of the angels] can *we* offer as music for tragedy?

9. *voids* (archaic): vanishes, dies.

13. *masque*: masquerade.

13–14. *tame/ My tempests . . .*: in *that* light how tame and fussy are my moods of despair and my feverish ardour!

PAGE 104. TO R.B. 22 April 1889. Hopkins's last poem, written six weeks before his death and addressed to Bridges.

6. *combs*: two possible meanings seem combined here: (1) straightens, orders—as with a comb. (2) stores—as in a honeycomb.

PAGE 104. THE WOODLARK. 5 July 1876. Hopkins left only fragments of this poem. The version here, published in *The Month*, June 1936, was rearranged by Fr. Geoffrey Bliss, S.J., who supplied the three lines given in square brackets so that the poem should not be spoilt by gaps.

20. *sash*: the soft sheaf of the wheat-ear.

23. *rudred* (archaic): rose-cheeked.

PAGE 106. ON THE PORTRAIT OF TWO BEAUTIFUL YOUNG PEOPLE. Monasterevan, Co. Kildare. Christmas 1886. The portrait which inspired the poem was of a brother and sister who lived near Monasterevan, where Hopkins spent Christmas 1886. He did not complete it and a year later wrote to Canon Dixon: 'I cannot get my Elegy finished, but I hope in a few days to see the hero and heroine of it, which may enable me (or quite the reverse; perhaps that: it is not well to come too near things).' But, as it stands, the poem seems a satisfying whole.

7. *In one fair fall*: i.e. in the birth of two beautiful children.

7. *for times overcast*: as for what the dark future has in store.

8. *heft* (dialect): effort, aspiration.

9–11. *The fine, the fingering beams* . . .: the fine, shaping lines of paint mirror and fix for ever.

12. *ringlet-race*: rush of dancing eddies.

12. *burling* (dialect): swirling. The Barrow flows past Monasterevan.

20. *stead*: help, steady.

22. *sways with*: influence (with secondary meaning, 'is in the balance with').

23–24. *a warning wavèd to* . . .: a reference to the young man of 'great possessions', who would not sell all and give to the poor and follow Jesus, to gain eternal life (Matt. xix. 16–22).

25. *list* (archaic): pleasure (with secondary meaning, 'tilt', 'precarious leaning').

25. *leaning*: bent, direction.

27–28. *The selfless self of self* . . .: the individual's ultimate selfhood. 'It is called "selfless" because it is "prior to nature", upon which it depends for its manifestation in being; it is "fast furled" and secret, for although its pitch of action is free, its destiny has been "foredrawn" by God: hence its full potentialities are unknown even to the person himself' (W. H. Gardner, *G. M. Hopkins*, I, 31 n.).

29. *Your feast of*: 'physical beauty' understood.

31. *Worst will the best*: it is the best who will do the worst.

PAGE 108. EPITHALAMION. Spring 1888. Written for his brother Everard's wedding in April 1888, but left unfinished. The fragments were arranged by Bridges.

4. *dean*: dene, valley.

4. *clough, cleave*: ravine.

9. *cover*: covert.

17. *huddling*: crowding together.

24. *fretty*: with fretted leaves.

25. *rafts*: dense flocks (perhaps as used of swimming birds).

36. *coffer*: boxed-in-pool.

37. *selfquainèd*: from 'quain', used by Hopkins as a form of 'quoin' (=coign), the external angle of a wall; hence to describe anything wedge-shaped, angular, fretted. Cf. Journal, p. 120.

27. *hoar-huskèd*: grey-covered.

38. *shives* (dialect): splinters, slices.

NOTES TO THE PROSE

PAGE III. OXFORD DIARIES.

9. *Lasher*: weir. A drawing of it is above the note.

63. *A day of the great mercy of God*: The religious crisis leading to this entry was followed by Hopkins's first recorded confession, on 25 March, and by his keeping of daily spiritual notes.

PAGE 115. THE JOURNAL.

1. *Addis*: William Edward Addis (1844–1917), of Balliol, one of Hopkins's most intimate Oxford friends. He became a Catholic just before Hopkins, but, after sixteen years as a priest, left the Roman Church, causing Hopkins very great pain. After a period as a Nonconformist minister, he returned to the Church of England. He published works on Church history.

157. *Bond*: Edward Bond (1844–1920), a close Oxford friend: he had given Hopkins great confidence on being shown some of his early poems. Later a barrister and Conservative M.P.

159. *inscaped*: For 'inscape', see Introduction, pp. 5–6.

160. *quains*: variant of 'quoins' (=coigns), wedge-shaped blocks; used also, below, of the angular points of a constellation. Cf. *Epithalamion*, l. 37: 'selfquainèd rocks'.

197. *purpurea candidior nive*: 'whiter than gleaming snow'.

330. *Agony in the Garden*: in *The Dolorous Passion of Our Lord Jesus Christ; from the Meditations of Anne Catherine Emmerich* (transl., 1862). Sister Emmerich (1774–1824) was a German Augustinian nun.

358. *Caesar's Camp*: a circular earthwork south of Wimbledon Common.

358. *squalentem*: dry, stiff.

417. *vows*: his first vows at the end of two years' probation as a novice.

513. *quaining*: see note on 'quains', above.

523. '*The young lambs bound . . .*': from Wordsworth's *Ode, Intimations of Immortality from Recollections of Early Childhood*, st. X.

614. *sidings*: i.e. modifications.

649. *Scotus on the Sentences*: *Scriptum Oxoniense*, his Commentary on the *Sentences* of Peter Lombard, 1514.

653. *Scotus*: see note to *Duns Scotus's Oxford* (p. 186) and Introduction, p. 8.

677. *Blandyke*: the Stonyhurst word for a monthly holiday, from Blandecques, a village near the Jesuit College at St. Omer, N. E. France, the ancestor of Stonyhurst.

678. *Lucas*: Herbert Lucas (1852–1933), Jesuit priest and writer.

698. *destroyed any more*: cf. *Binsey Poplar*.

762. *Douglas*: in the Isle of Man.

799. *fatiscebat*: gaped open.

811. θυμός: life.

848. *Bishopsteignton*: in Devonshire.

850. *Weeping Winifred*: a popular tune.

864. *comes home*: Cf. *The Starlight Night*.

865. *Kerr*: William Hobart Kerr (1836–1913), who had entered the Jesuit novitiate a year before Hopkins.

866. *behind ours*: Hopkins had come to St. Beuno's College, near St. Asaph, N. Wales, to study theology, on 28 August. He described it in a letter to his father the next day: ' . . . The garden is all heights, terraces, Excelsiors, misty mountain tops, seats up trees called Crows' Nests, flights of steps seemingly up to heaven lined with burning aspiration upon aspiration of scarlet geraniums.'

882. *to learn Welsh*: W. H. Gardner's publication of Hopkins's *Cywydd* of 24 April 1876 (*Poems*, 3rd edn., p. 190) shows that he had made considerable progress in Welsh by then. He almost certainly also wrote a Welsh version of the Latin hymn *O Deus, ego amo te* (*Poems*, p. 189). Of the effect of Welsh poetry on his own he wrote to both Bridges and Dixon (see p. 159). Its influence on his poetic technique is discussed by Gweneth Lilly in *Modern Language Review*, July 1943, pp. 192–205, and by W. H. Gardner, *G. M. Hopkins*, II, 143–57.

895. *rules of election*: the rules governing the choice of a state of life, laid down in the *Spiritual Exercises* of St. Ignatius Loyola.

PAGE 144. COMMENTS ON THE SPIRITUAL EXERCISES OF ST. IGNATIUS LOYOLA.

St. Ignatius Loyola (1491–1556) was the Spanish founder of the Society of Jesus, an order bound by vows of chastity, poverty, and obedience, and originally dedicated to support the Roman Catholic Church against the Reformation. Study and practice of his *Spiritual Exercises* are the basis of a Jesuit's spiritual training.

Principium sive Fundamentum: 'The Principle or Foundation.' Meditation upon it is commonly referred to as the 'Foundation Exercise'. Hopkins's comments are written in an interleaved copy of the text.

12. *more hold*: 'Although this treatise is the most richly individual of all GMH's writings, yet several of his arguments spring from positions that are distinctively Scotist as opposed to Thomist. This

preference for introspection is the first instance. Scotus's proof of the existence of God dispenses with evidence from the outside world and derives solely from the existence of one finite being (one's self) endowed with mind and will' (Christopher Devlin, S.J., *Sermons and Devotional Writings*, p. 283).

32. *taste of myself*: here and throughout this passage cf. *Henry Purcell*.

PAGE 146. LETTERS.
To A. W. M. Baillie, 10 July 1863. Alexander William Mowbray Baillie (1843–1921), a rationalist Scot, was an intimate friend of Hopkins at Balliol. He became a barrister but, after a visit to Egypt for his health, devoted most of his life to his interests in Egyptian archaeology and language: subjects on which he and Hopkins corresponded at length from 1886 to 1888. They had a great affection for each other.

17. *Epimenidicularly*: presumably, according to the Cretan poet and prophet Epimenides (sixth cent. B.C.).

PAGE 147. *To A. W. M. Baillie, 10 September 1864.*
51. *the Hexameron*: an Oxford High Church essay society.
93. *tropical island*: ll. 572–80.
171. *In Memoriam*: CXXI. 'Sad Hesper . . .'
189. *Wordsworth*: the end of the sonnet 'Composed near Calais, on the road leading to Ardres, August 7, 1802' (published 1807). The lines originally ran:

> Yet despair
> I feel not: happy am I as a Bird:
> Fair seasons yet will come, and hopes as fair.

The change was made in 1827.
198. *Milman*: Henry Hart Milman (1791–1868), Dean of St. Paul's. He wrote several long dramatic poems.

PAGE 152. *To Robert Bridges, 2 August 1871.* Robert Seymour Bridges (1844–1930), Hopkins's most intimate friend, went up to Corpus Christi, Oxford, from Eton. He practised as a doctor until 1882, then devoted himself to writing. He was appointed Poet Laureate in 1913. He and Hopkins corresponded until Hopkins's death, after which Bridges preserved all his friend's mature poems and edited the first complete edition in 1918. His best known work now is *The Testament of Beauty*, 1929.
228. *Shooting Niagara*: in *Macmillan's Magazine*, 1867.

PAGE 154. *To Robert Bridges, 21 August 1877.*
312. '*lashed: rod*': *Wreck of the Deutschland*, st. 2, l. 2.

PAGE 157. *To Robert Bridges, 13 May 1878.*
341. *Eurydice*: *The Loss of the Eurydice*.
341. *The Month*: the Jesuit journal. Its editor, Fr. Henry Coleridge, great-nephew of S. T. Coleridge, had also rejected *The Wreck of the Deutschland*.
354. '*If it were done when 'tis done*': *Macbeth*, I. vii. 1.

PAGE 158. *To R. W. Dixon, 5 October 1878.* Richard Watson Dixon (1833–1900), Anglican clergyman, poet and historian, had been at Oxford a close friend of Burne-Jones, Morris, and others of the Pre-Raphaelite Brotherhood. During 1861 he taught at Highgate, where he met Hopkins. He was now a Canon of Carlisle. He responded joyfully to Hopkins's first letter praising his poems, in June 1878, and intensely admired Hopkins's own poetry (see Introduction, p. 14).
448. '. . . *prívate retúrned*': the last line of *Paradise Regained*.
450. '. . . *héllish wiles*': *op. cit.*, I, 175.

PAGE 161. *To R. W. Dixon, 27 February 1879.*
480. '*primrosed and hung with shade*': 'Regeneration' (*Silex Scintillans*).
482. '*The lilies of his love appear*': 'The Revival' (*Thalia Rediviva*).
527. '*before the time*': *Harold* (1876).

PAGE 163. *To Robert Bridges, 22 April 1879.*
534. *Lang's*: Andrew Lang (1844–1912), poet and scholar.
535. *the Odyssey*: with S. H. Butcher, 1879.
550. *Mr. Gosse*: Edmund Gosse (1849–1928), scholar, critic, and poet; knighted in 1925. Hopkins nicknamed him 'the habitually joyous'.

PAGE 164. *To R. W. Dixon, 12 October 1881.*
557. *Lothair*: Disraeli's novel, 1870.
576. '*carried away with their dissimulation*': Gal. ii. 13.

PAGE 165. *To Coventry Patmore, 6 October 1886.* Coventry Kersey Dighton Patmore (1823–96), poet and Roman Catholic convert, had met Hopkins at Stonyhurst in July 1883. He greatly admired him; treated Hopkins's detailed criticism of his poems with the greatest respect; but did not understand Hopkins's own poetry. His best known poem is *The Angel in the House*, 1854–6, a celebration of marital love.
610. *Barnes*: William Barnes (1801–86), the Dorset dialect poet.
635. *I could do that better*: see note on Hopkins's use of Welsh poetic techniques, p. 203.

636. *Paladore and Polly dear*: from *Poems of Rural Life in the Dorset Dialect*, Third Collection, 1862.

PAGE 167. *To R. W. Dixon, 23 October 1886.*

659. *Wordsworth's ode*: *Intimations of Immortality from Recollections of Early Childhood*.

PAGE 169. *To Coventry Patmore, 20 October 1887.*

730. *a St. James's Gazette*: the issue of 28 June 1887. The review is reprinted in Patmore's *Principle in Art*, 1889.

732. *Keats:* Sir Sidney Colvin, *Keats*, 1887 (English Men of Letters series).

772. *that must be bound*: 'This precious book of love, this unbound lover,/ To beautify him, only lacks a cover' (I. iii. 88–89).

775. *something good lately*: the Preface to the selection from Keats in Ward's *English Poets*, Vol. IV, 1880; reprinted in *Essays in Criticism*, Second Series, 1888.

PAGE 172. *To Coventry Patmore, 6 May 1888.*

820. *'O for a life . . .'*: 'However it may be, O for a Life of Sensations rather than of Thoughts!' (letter to Bailey, 22 November 1817).

PAGE 174. *To Robert Bridges, 25 September 1888.*

894. *Fire*: *That Nature is a Heraclitean Fire and of the Comfort of the Resurrection.*

925. *Statistics and Free Will*: Hopkins's paper did not appear.

928. *my war-song*: the music for his poem, '*What shall I do for the land that bred me*' (*Poems*, 3rd edn., p. 168).